Estelle Popham   Blanche Ettinger

ABOUT THE AUTHORS

Estelle Popham received her bachelor's degree in English from the University of Wisconsin, an M.A. degree in business from Iowa State University, and a Ph.D. in business education from New York University. She has taught business subjects at the high school, business school, and college levels, and was named by the National Business Education Association as the outstanding business educator of 1976. Dr. Popham is active in professional associations and has co-authored five books on business-related topics.

Blanche Ettinger received her B.A. and M.S. degrees in education from Hunter College of the City University of New York and is now a doctoral candidate at New York University. She has worked as a secretary, taught at the high school l   ̀ ̀ currently an associate professo   the Department of Secretarial Studi College of the Ci Mrs. Ettinger is a Xi Chapter of I graduate business education fraternity, and past president of the Secretarial Educators of the State University of New York.

OPPORTUNITIES IN
OFFICE OCCUPATIONS

ESTELLE L. POPHAM
BLANCHE ETTINGER

Vocational Guidance Manuals
A Division of Data Courier, Inc.
Louisville, Kentucky

Publisher—Loene Trubkin
Editor—Christine Maddox
Assistant Editor—Betty Unruh
Photo Editor—Donna Lawrence
Production Manager—Carmen Chetti
Production Supervisor—Sylvia Ward
Administrative Services—Cynthia Pierce

Manufactured in the
United States of America

Revised Edition

Library of Congress Catalog Card Number 76—14061

ISBN Number   0-89022-219-3 (Hardcover)
               0-89022-052-2 (Paperbound)

ABOUT THE AUTHORS

ESTELLE L. POPHAM was graduated from the University of Wisconsin with a major in English; but then, as today, there were few teaching positions available. She was forced by economic necessity to enroll at a local business college. What was at the time a major disappointment turned into what she describes as "the best thing that ever happened to me." This experience opened up an understanding of the many opportunities in the office occupations, and she wonders, "Why didn't somebody tell me earlier about the business field?"

Her own experience is the primary reason for her later interest in writing a vocational guidance manual to acquaint young people with the various kinds of entry-level (and later) jobs.

Doctor Popham became a business teacher and has taught at every level—high school, business school, and college in Missouri, Pennsylvania, North Carolina, and New York. She is now professor emeritus at Hunter College of The City University of New York. She received an M.A. degree in business from the Iowa State University and a Ph.D. in business education from New York University.

She has been very active in professional associations: vice president of the Eastern Business Education Association, sponsor of Delta Pi Epsilon (honorary graduate business education fraternity) at Hunter College, member of the board of the National Business Education Association, member of the committee to plan and lead the American Management Association's seminars for executive secretaries, editor of the yearbook of the National Business Education Association, and member of the

New York Personnel Association and The Supervisors and Administrators Association. She is a former dean of the Institute for Certifying Secretaries.

Publications (all with co-authors) include seven editions of *Secretarial Procedures And Administration,* two editions of *Gregg Speedbuilding For Colleges,* three editions of *Methods Of Teaching Business Subjects, Filing And Records Management, A Teaching-Learning System For Business Education,* and three previous editions of *Opportunities In Office Occupations.*

In recognition of accomplishments during a long career in business education, in 1976 at the national convention of the National Business Education Association, Doctor Popham received the John R. Gregg Award as outstanding business educator. That same year she was named Teacher of the Year by the Business Education Association of New York City.

BLANCHE ETTINGER is an associate professor in the Department of Secretarial Studies at Bronx Community College of The City University of New York. She formerly taught on the high school level; prior to that, she was secretary to the executive vice-president of Cohn Hall Marx Company.

She received her B.A. degree and M.S. in education from Hunter College of The City University of New York and is now a doctoral candidate at New York University, where she has taken many courses in guidance and occupational information.

Mrs. Ettinger is a past president of the Alpha Xi Chapter of Delta Pi Epsilon (honorary graduate business education fraternity) and also a past president of the Secretarial Educators of the State University of New York. She is an Executive Committee member of the New York State Association of Junior Colleges as well as her college representative. For her outstanding service to this organization for almost a decade, Mrs. Ettinger was awarded a certificate of recognition.

Her professional activities are numerous: editor of the *1977 Journal* of the Business Education Association of Metropolitan

New York; National Council Delegate of the Alpha Xi Chapter, Delta Pi Epsilon; and member of the Eastern Business Education Association, New York State Business Teachers Association, Supervisors and Administrators Association, National Business Education Association, and the International Society of Business Educators.

Among her publications are *Exploring Business Occupational Information,* "Parent Counseling and Conferences," and "Teaching and Learning Approaches to Secretarial Studies." She has participated in many professional meetings as a speaker and panelist.

TABLE OF CONTENTS

Help wanted. Opinions of business leaders. Effect of automation on clerical demand. Automated communication of numbers and words. Projections for 1985. The minorities and disadvantaged. Changes in age and sex of clerical workers. Classifications of workers in the clerical occupations. Job titles and descriptions.

Changing activities of the clerk. What skills are important? Educational preparation. Community colleges. Company training. Other training programs. Abilities required in tomorrow's offices. How to get started. The working situation. Part-time and temporary employment. Disadvantages. Promotion opportunities for clerks. Types of machines commonly operated by clerks.

Employment and salaries. Educational requirements. How former students view their training in records management.

LIST OF CHARTS

PREFACE

This fourth edition of *Opportunities In Office Occupations,* first published in 1958, will reflect many changes that have been dictated by the dynamics of our times. Facts and statistics have been brought up to date, several sections have been completely rewritten, and new chapters have been added on processing words, processing data, and records management.

This book is a source of vocational guidance information for the students who should be aware of the opportunities available to them in the business world not only for today but tomorrow too. Office occupations are described, the duties and requirements of the job, the educational preparation needed, the work situation, and the employment trends and earnings.

The masculine pronouns are being used in this book for succinctness and are intended to refer to both females and males.

INTRODUCTION

The character of many existing office positions has changed, new office functions have been created, job titles are now non-sexist and no longer referred to as a man's job or a woman's job. These changes occurred as a result of our technological explosion, the demand for faster communications, the ever-increasing reporting demanded by the government and regulatory agencies, economic conditions, legislation, and affirmative action. What has been the impact of some of these factors?

As more and more firms began to use computers and automated business machines, the demand for the routine and unskilled clerical worker such as payroll clerk, general clerk, and file clerk decreased; prospects became best in those clerical occupations which developed as a result of the new technologies or which were not affected by automation. The Bureau of Labor Statistics predicts that, by the mid-1980s, more than 80 percent of today's jobs will require technical specialization and a high level of skill requirements. The better-trained individual with occupational skills has an advantage in the job market today. Job opportunities are especially favorable for secretaries, typists, receptionists, and computer operators. An example of how a machine can replace a low-level clerk is occurring at Citibank in New York. The job of mail clerk is being replaced by a Mailmobile, a driverless robot mail carrier that is programmed to travel a certain route, making stops at particular stations for a designated length of time to deliver the mail, paperwork, and supplies.

The Equal Pay Act of 1963 and its subsequent amendments prohibiting discrimination on the basis of sex, race, or color led to affirmative action programs beyond the establishment of neutral "non-discriminatory" and "merit-hiring" policies. Because of affirmative action, many women and minorities moved into positions for which they were well qualified and which were previously held by males. Promotional opportunities became unusually good, and access to training programs for upward mobility became available. According to the Research Institute of America, the year of the breakthrough for women was 1972. Women represent 46.7 percent of today's workers in all fields, an increase of 21.7 percent from the 25 percent employed in 1940. What are some of the reasons for this increase? Affirmative action, described previously; open enrollment in colleges (guaranteed admission for all high school graduates); the changing role expectations of women; the expansion of fields in which women can expect jobs; changes in child-bearing patterns; the changing philosophy of the role of the family breadwinner; and our inflationary economy which requires more earning power to support a household. Statistics show a positive correlation between the educational level achieved by women and the percentage of women working. Today, society no longer frowns upon a woman who remains single and seeks a career or combines a career and marital responsibilities; in fact, there is growing value for doing "one's own thing." In some of our largest organizations, the number of women managers has increased, partly in response to the need to fill the gap for managerial help.

The recession, which gathered momentum in late 1974 and 1975, led to cutbacks in overstaffed organizations and contributed to the high unemployment rate. The loss of jobs was especially severe for men, and a comparison of the decline in employment between men and women is revealing. The employment of women decreased to a lesser extent and began to rise much sooner. Statistics show that even in the face of rising unemployment, the number of women in the labor force increased substantially in 1975. The demand for the temporary worker to perform the special tasks required periodically by business and industry also rose. A survey conducted during the low point in the recession that examined unemployment in relation to the level of an individual's formal education indicated that the jobless rate for high school dropouts was 15.2 percent; for high school graduates, 9.1 percent; for those with some college training, 6.9 percent; and for college graduates, 2.9 percent. These figures suggest that the demand for college graduates is expected to grow at three times the rate of the demand for all workers in the American labor force.

Patterns of employment and unemployment have shifted throughout the nation with the relocation of major business and industrial firms. For example, because of deteriorating conditions in New York City and the tax structure, some of Manhattan's most prestigious corporate firms relocated to other cities or to the suburbs, with a resulting loss of thousands of positions in the office sector. Many cities, especially those in the Northeast, reflect the same trend.

One area showing a gain in employment opportunities throughout the country is banking. In New York City alone, 14,000 jobs were added between 1970-1976, of which 4,000 were in 1975. Banking was the third largest source of job growth, surpassed only by local government and medical and other health services.

Another factor for change in office positions and the labor force is the newer approach in education. A glance at some of the recent educational philosophies will show how schools and work form a cohesive bond not only for earning a living but for living a life.

One such philosophy is continuing education. As society changes, so must people so that they will not become obsolete and sterile. Through continuing education programs in the schools today, communities are fulfilling a commitment to their citizens for lifelong learning. Young people and adults of all ages have opportunities for further study in the humanities, for job improvement, for the acquisition of basic consumer and economic knowledges, for the development of personal-use skills, for retraining and for reentering the job market, for recreation, and for self-improvement.

Another concept is career education, initially proposed by Sidney Marland, former U.S. Commissioner of Education. Career education prepares a person to lead a useful, productive, and self-fulfilling lifestyle of his or her own choice. The concept is much broader than mere vocational education. Students are prepared academically, emotionally, and practically to enable them to function in life, with its changes and its ups and downs. Career education starts with the very young child and continues at all levels of learning. Individuals receive direction in clarifying their values and interests, develop the ability to make decisions, and become aware of occupational information and lifestyles.

With these ideas in mind, you will understand the changes that have occurred in office occupations, the expanding range of occupations available to young people today, and the future trends. You will be able to make wiser career decisions while reading this analysis of office jobs for which you can qualify and to which you can match your personal talents, interests, and values.

Chapter 1

THE OPPORTUNITIES

The job search is a planned, carefully structured process that leads to wise decision making in the choice of an occupation. One important step is to obtain accurate and up-to-date information on employment opportunities. Listed below are typical want ads appearing in the current newspapers. These "Help Wanted" advertisements indicate the range of jobs that exist for individuals with secretarial and/or clerical skills and give some idea about the prevailing salaries for specific positions. The discussion that follows in this book analyzes the various occupations defining the nature of the work, the educational requirements, the skill and personal qualifications needed, and the future outlook for employment. Suggestions are given for ways to prepare for office positions.

HELP WANTED

SECY $8/8,500
AIRLINES
Travel benefits. Good skills req.
No phone calls will be accepted.
CORNWALL agency 179 Bway
349-2520

Mag Card II Ops, Fee Pd $185
MAJOR PARK AVE LAW FIRM!!
4 WKS VAC! NO LEGAL EXP OK!
ALLEN agency 15 E 40, 532-9100

KEYPUNCH OPR
For Keypunch and lt clerical, $150/wk, 35 hr wk. Call for appt 982-7880, attn Jim Smith

EXECUTIVE
SECRETARY
To Chairman of the Board of professional corporation. Excellent typing & steno skills required. Personable. Upper midtown-E side loc. Salary open.
CALL 421-1634

ACCOUNTING CLERK
Wall ST. firm with diversified accounting office needs person with good typing and phone manner plus knowledge of adding machine. Primary responsibilities process invoices for payment, draw checks and post G/L on Burroughs L5000. No prior bookkeeping machine experience required. Good fringe benefits. Contact Mr. Kohan 623-2211.

TYPIST
Publisher requires accurate typist to work in typing pool in production area. Good spelling ability and work exp required. 50 wpm. UN area. Hours 8:30 to 4PM. All benefits. Mr. Lucas 644-7625.
An equal opportunity employer

TEMPORARY   NO FEE
TRANSCRIBERS
1-3 FULL DAYS OR LONGER
DOT SERVICES
150 Broadway (Nr Wall) Rm. 911
TEL: 227-5000
Dot Personnel Services, Inc.
A Subsidiary of Dictaphone Corp.

BOOKKEEPER
PAYROLL CLERK
Experienced data processing, accounts payable. Excellent company benefits. Send resume stating salary requirements to:
Y6364 TIMES
an equal opportunity employer

SECY   FEE PD   to $180
DICTAPHONE
VP of Blue Chip firm needs articulate, personable indiv to asst him. Gd typg & ability to work on own nec. Excel benefits & bonuses.
Call Rita DeSilvio   349-3610
WILLIAM HARRIS agency
150 Bway

ADMIN SECRETARY
INTERNATIONALLY–KNOWN
ARCHITECTURAL FIRM
for office & business development directors. Gd secretarial skills req'd. Excel oppty + benefits.
Call Mrs. Brody on Tuesday
751-1540
Equal Opportunity Employer

ADMIN./ASST.
$10,000 + FEE PAID
-T.V. STUDIO-

Assistant to producer of popular T.V. show. Get involved with cast & production work at major studio. Min. 2+ years exp. working for a producer and gd. skills. (spdwtg, o.k.) Call/see J. Gordon first thing tomorrow. Key Agency 130 E. 40 St. 11 Fl. 689-2300.

BILLING SECY To $15M+

Co Pays Fee + Bonus + Benefits Spanish/Engl, gd skills, work with chief fincl ofcr, banking exper. Kling Agency 180 Bwy NY
964-3640

STAT TYPIST-STENO
EXP MIDTOWN CPA FIRM
PERMANENT FRINGE
BENEFITS.

SAL OPEN.   564-8005

OFFICE CLERK
ACCURATE TYPING

Good at figures, telephone. West 22nd Street. Call 675-4097.

BOOKKEEPER

Wall St law firm seeks qualified person to administer internal operns. Excel sal & fringe bnfts, permanent position. Please call 684-6202.

VYDEC OP $180-210

Major Midtown "Oil Co" has several openings. Will consider trainee with life experience and good typing or experienced operators. Superior benefits program.

GAL/GUY FRIDAY

Energetic humorous, responsible, enthusiastic person for small fantastic young textile design firm, excel bnfts, working cond, long hrs, lo pay quick advancement for right person. Must type. Upr E side 879-3100.

DATA
PROCESSING DIRECTOR

Northern Virginia based NYSE chain retail company seeks an experienced Data Processing Director to head major installation. Retail experience desired in IBM 360/370 systems. This is an attractive growth opportunity with excellent salary, bonus and benefits. Submit resume in confidence to:

Box P-768, Wall Street Journal

MAG CARD
WORD PROCESSING

IWD COMPLETE Word Processing Service Bureau/Placement Center offers oppty to train on premises. We need opers, admin support team for all magnetic key boards. Vydec, Xerox 800, Mag I, Mag II. Must type 50 WPM.

MS BEA-Intl Word Data 964-6744

Word Processing is our only biz

COMPUTER OPERATOR
TO $10,400
International travel co. seeks high school grad with min 1 yrs. exp on IBM 370/115, 370/125, 370/135 or 370/145 (DOS/VS). Applicant must also have exp in master file updating & batch processing & be willing to rotate shifts on a 3 month basis. Please submit resume and salary history to Box 979-B, 15 E. 41 St, NY 11017 An equal opportunity employer M/F

ADMINISTRATIVE ASST
As the head of a rapidly growing manufacturing company, I need a bright, conscientious individual to be my assistant. Duties to include inventory control, order follow-up, office supervision & special projects: Y6117 TIMES

P/T Proofreader for CPA ofc Must have knowledge of form of financial statements. Other duties incl light bkkpg, computer work, approx 25 hr per week. Call 889-4242

MEDICAL RECEPT F/T
Volume practice. Greenwich Vill. Exp pfd. Salary negotiable. 4 full days. Call Mon, Tues, Thurs, Fri between 1-3pm & Wed betwn 11-2pm. 228-5601.

TYPIST STATISTICAL
Acctg firm, small ofc W 57 St. Expd to take charge of ofc duties & steno. Salary open. Permanent. 246-3507

RECEPTIONIST
publshng co needs gd typist, pleasant voice, must be expd & must be neat. Call Tues aft 10AM Carol 535-6100

TYPIST/SWITCHBOARD
Good typist, dictaphone, relief console switchboard, mail distribution, telex. Front desk appearance a must. Lite exp considered. Excel salary & benefits. Midtown area. Call 682-8158

TYPISTS-DICTAPHONE
Great demand for qualified individuals. Hi Salary. Full or Part time. Call 377-7588 for appt.

ACCOUNTANT JR
Min 1 yr exp with small CPA firm car nec. Box 121 Baldwin NY 11510.

CLERK – Good at Figures
Good oppty for mature person. General office work, order processing, check invoices etc. No typing Well estab firm. Call Miss Cassella at 924-8888

TEMPORARY
Pay On Fri.   NO FEE
SECRETARIES START
AT $4.50 per hour
Minimum steno 90 wpm
STEAD-FAST Temp
160 Bway, 374-1140

At some time or other, most people hold some sort of clerical position in an office. It may be for the summer while the worker is in high school or college; it may be part-time after school in the afternoon; it may be full-time and the ultimate career of the worker; or it may be a part-time job for the housewife whose family responsibilities permit work outside the home only a few hours a week. Even if you are interested in a clerical position just for the summer or for part of the day, you can eliminate a lot of waste motion by getting facts about the jobs in clerical occupations. Whether you are contemplating a long-term career or working as clerk just for the time being, the only intelligent approach to the job is to consider its opportunities and limitations.

In 1972, the U.S. Bureau of Labor Statistics reported that 14.2 million people or 17.4 percent of the total number employed were clerical workers. By April, 1974, the figure rose to over 15 million or 17.9 percent. Office workers represent the largest employment group in the United States.

The clerical field is one of the largest single occupational groups among women today. Approximately two out of every five American workers employed full-time are women, and the biggest contribution to the growth of the labor force in recent years came from women. By April, 1976, over 1.2 million women were added to the labor force; the adult female participation is now up to 46.7 percent (or 37.8 million) contrasted with 39 percent in 1970 (or 30 million) and 23 percent in 1920. (See Chart 1.) Of the 15.5 million persons employed as clerical workers during April, 1976, 4.6 million were working as secretaries, stenographers, typists; the other 10.8 million were employed as clerical workers.*

Employment and Earnings, U.S. Department of Labor, Bureau of Labor Statistics (Washington, D.C.: May, 1976).

CHART 1

Percentage of Employed Women (16 years and over) in Labor Force
1960-1976

Percentage of Employed Women in Clerical Occupations
1960-1976

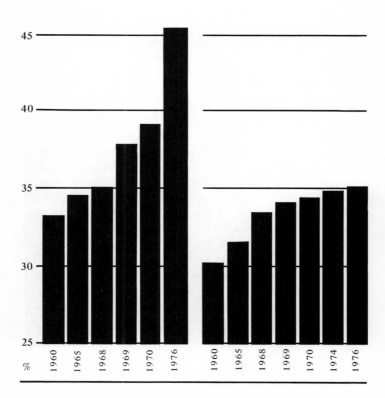

CHART 2

**Percentage of Employed Men and Women
Clerical Workers (16 years and over)
in Labor Force**
1960-1985*

*based on data from
  U.S. Department of Labor

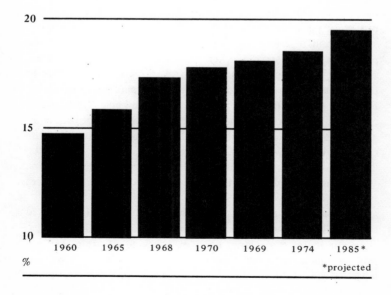

| | 1960 | 1965 | 1968 | 1970 | 1969 | 1974 | 1985* |

%   *projected

The outlook for office workers during the 1970s and 1980s shows continuing growth. Between 1900 and 1950, office employment increased 725 percent; between 1950 and 1960, 32 percent; and by 1975, was 17 percent above 1969 levels. Estimates indicate that clerical employment will grow considerably faster than total employment, increasing to 19.8 million in 1985 or 19.4 percent of the total labor force. (See Chart 2.) Projections for the annual rate of growth indicate a one percent slowdown in 1980-1985 (1.9 percent) in comparison to 1972-1980 (2.9 percent) because of the anticipated decrease in the rate of growth of trade and manufacturing, which employed approximately one-third of all clerical workers in 1972. However, it is significant that this decline is less for clerical workers than for most other occupational groups.

The projected increase in clerical demand is a result of the rapid growth in size and complexity of business organization, particularly in banking, finance, insurance, real estate, and professional service organizations.

Although technological innovations decrease employment opportunities for clerical workers in jobs such as payroll, filing, customer billing, and inventory control, there was an increase in the number of clerical workers needed to prepare the information flow for computers. Secretaries, stenographers, typists, and receptionists are some of the categories that should not be greatly affected by computer installations. In fact, half the growth in the clerical group between 1972 and 1985, or 2.5 million, is from the demand for the increased use of secretaries, stenographers, typists, and receptionists in business services and legal services industries.

This manual is designed to give some concept of the vast field of clerical work—what kinds of jobs are involved, the qualifications for them, the salaries paid, the working situation, and the promotional possibilities. Hopefully this book will give those who have only a vague notion about a "job in an office" a simple realistic discussion of the clerical field. With an insight into the kinds of jobs available, the principal duties involved, the effect of technological changes on job classifications, the training necessary for clerical work, and promotional opportunities, readers may be motivated either for or against securing a position in clerical work, the fastest-growing occupational field in the United States.

Business is based on countless written paper records of facts and figures. The preparation and maintenance of these records require millions of man-hours annually. Those who specialize in their handling are generally known as clerks. There are many kinds of clerks. A clerk who does many kinds of office work is a general clerk. A clerk who does a particular kind of office work is a specialized clerk. Some specialized clerical jobs are those of typist, receptionist, file clerk, bookkeeper, stenographer, cashier, postal clerk, shipping and receiving clerk, statistical clerk, stock clerk, and office machine operator (duplicator operator, calculator operator, keypunch operator, and voice-writing equipment operator). Although the names of the jobs of specialized clerks do not always include the word *clerk*, they actually fall into the clerical classification of office jobs. The clerical field, as defined by the Department of Labor, covers a wide range of office occupations from messenger to the highly skilled positions of title searcher and examiner, executive secretary, or office manager with professional certification. This manual will consider the overall development of the clerical field and then discuss in detail the job of general and special clerk—with special chapters devoted to the work of the word processors (stenographers and correspondence and administrative secretaries), data processors (bookkeepers, accounting clerks, computer operators), and records managers.

OPINIONS OF BUSINESS LEADERS

Several business leaders were asked for their opinions of vocational opportunities for clerical workers and for suggestions to those considering positions in the field. Through their statements runs a common understanding of the great need for qualified clerical workers with good attitudes.

Paul J. Riordan, district marketing manager for Delta Airlines in Louisville, Kentucky, forecasts good career opportunities in the future for multi-talented clerical workers:

> "During my 45 years in the aviation industry, I have seen the importance of competent clerical help increase 1,000 percent. Many years ago, clerical workers were expected to do only filing and incidental work in offices. Today, in addition to those duties, clerks are expected to perform a variety of other, more complex duties. For example, they may be required to understand the workings of computers and may be called upon to analyze readouts or to help their supervisors interpret information generated by machines. In the airline industry, it is not unusual for a clerk to be required to interpret at least nine different readouts in their entirety. From this, you can see that it is a misnomer to classify such office personnel as *clerks,* even though clerical duties may be an important part of their jobs.
>
> Today, clerical workers are given more latitude and opportunities for advancement than ever before. Office personnel who have good skills, the right attitudes toward their jobs, innovative minds, ambition to improve, and the ability to change when change is necessary will find themselves rising to meet stimulating challenges in modern offices."

The president of the New York Chamber of Commerce, Mr. Thomas N. Stainback, sees a bright future for young people who are interested in clerical vocations and who have the necessary skills, habits, and desire. He states:

"As the operations officer of a business association which numbers some 2,000 corporate and individual members in the New York City area, I can state that vocational opportunities for clerical workers, both male and female, are and will continue to be strong in our economy. Even at a time of business downturn and recovery, this is the prospect because modern business is conducted by means of reports, letters, memoranda, minutes of meetings, orders, instructions, manuals, and records—in short, through the written word and the written figures.

"Whether it be the largest of corporations—and New York City has one-quarter of the nation's largest firms headquartered here—or the smallest of offices, business depends on office workers who can carry out their duties competently.

"An individual business will give specialized training to the extent necessary to its own operations. But an individual business must have something to work with, and it must build on the skills and habits already acquired by the prospective employee in his or her own high school or college education. That this "educating process" is not always satisfactory is attested to by the experience of any number of companies, which report that *on the average* they have to hire and try out four clerical employees in order to find the one person who can bring with him or her the skills, habits, and willingness to work which are required to do and keep the job.

"In our competitive economic system, a business can survive and prosper only if it has competent people up and down the line, from beginning secretary to the president, who can contribute to the total operation.

"Businesses in this day and age recognize that there are students who, through no fault of their own, have not had full educational opportunity and that there is an obligation by business to help make the students employable. Businesses in New York City do this by supporting Street Academies, through consortium clerical training by bringing relevance to school curricula and by conducting on-the-job remedial training, where needed, to enable the willing employee to keep and progress in his job. In this Chamber over the past five years, we have trained for member firms over 1,200 young people from minority and disadvantaged backgrounds. It's been an exciting and fulfilling program.

"As our economy becomes even more service-oriented, the future is bright for young people who want to work in the various clerical vocations offered by corporations, banks, insurance companies, utilities, educational institutions, and government. They have but to accept the challenge for a rewarding experience."

Dr. Irene Place, professor emeritus of business at Portland State College and an active member of many committees in business management organizations, such as Administrative Management Society and Association for Systems Management, emphasizes that many specialized clerical positions are available but that educational requirements are changing. Dr. Place states:

"The office function in business and government contains many interesting employment opportunities for young people, but educational requirements are changing. Clerical jobs where one did a little filing, a little typing, a little duplicating, and perhaps relieved the switchboard operator a few hours each day have changed because clerical positions, like other office positions, have been affected by new office machines, such as instant copiers, automated and microfilmed files, programmed typewriters, and by computers.

"The term clerical worker is now rarely used in business. Clerical work has been divided into specializations which are given such titles as programmer, console operator, records librarian, tape librarian, keypunch operator, and computer room operator, to name a few. As offices become larger and more mechanized, specialization grows. The general clerk—a jack of all trades—is becoming extinct.

"To be a specialist, one must focus on a particular cluster of skills and knowledges. If you want to work in an electronic computer center, you must learn about information flow systems, data "banks," and programming. You must learn about input/output devices.

"Not to be overlooked, however, because of the glamour of new job titles and specialization, is the importance of old, basic fundamentals when preparing for employment. The fundamentals—reading, writing, and arithmetic—are still important. Do you understand what you *read?* Can you *write* a clear instruction? Can you do simple *arithmetic* accurately? Are you dependable? Can you express yourself clearly? Do you have an agreeable, pleasant appearance and behavior? Do you use good judgment? Do you get along with people? Do they enjoy working with you?

"Getting work done accurately, dependably, and with a minimum of frustration and tension is still important where people work together. Yes, office jobs have changed during the past decade, and office equipment has become more automatic. There are new office job titles. The people, however, who work in offices are not too different from those of yesteryear. There still is no substitute for dependability, judgment, cheerfulness, and competence. If you have a good background, you can get results and move ahead in your occupational field. Confucius say, "Man like tack; go as far as head permits."

Mr. Donald L. Fruehling, vice president of McGraw-Hill Book Company, focuses on another qualification—the ability to adjust to change. He explains:

"In this decade as in the past, the fastest-growing occupations are those that require technical training. By 1980, it is predicted that there will be as many professional and technical workers as blue-collar workers; and the clerical occupations with more than 17 million workers will be larger than any other occupational group.

"These occupational and industrial growth trends will mean that the office worker of the future will need to adjust to a constantly changing work environment. Of course, it will still be necessary to develop those technical skills, such as typewriting, transcription, accounting, and computing; however, the real opportunity for the clerical worker of the future will depend on how well he is able to cultivate the habits, attitudes, and interests that relate to learning, adjusting, and advancing on a job. The clerical worker who has developed this ability to adjust will be a candidate for the more challenging and interesting positions in the office of the future."

These statements indicate that some types of clerical positions will continue to increase in number—even with office work becoming more and more mechanized and automatic. A clerk can be assured of employment for a long time to come, and for the highly competent, there will be opportunities for advancement to higher clerical positions and to supervisory and administrative positions in the clerical area.

EFFECT OF AUTOMATION ON CLERICAL DEMAND

In these days of great scientific and technological advances, probably no word can cause more excitement than "automation." This word is of interest to businessmen, educators, youngsters still in school, and all those in the labor force—the employed and unemployed.

Those not informed about automation envision themselves as being replaced by a mechanical monster which will take away their jobs. They forget, or are unaware of the fact, that the computer must be told what to do and how to do it. The brain of the human being is behind every piece of mechanical genius; human beings are responsible for the development of systems and procedures that will utilize the capabilities of the machines for maximum efficiency.

Automation is not something new. Technological changes have been occurring in human civilization ever since the invention of the wheel. Despite the increased efficiency from these technological improvements that make it possible to increase production with fewer workers, the Bureau of Labor Statistics estimates that by 1985 there will be 19 million more persons gainfully employed than at present. This increase in employment will be caused by the growth in population and the growing need for services. Most of the technological changes have created new opportunities, new comforts, and new possibilities for better, safer, and less-painful living.

It is true, however, that automation is bringing, and will continue to bring, great changes which will demand adjustment on the part of both the employer and the worker. The federal government, business, and schools are cooperating to make this transition as easy as possible for those presently employed and for you, the workers of tomorrow.

Automated machines, including the computer, have increased employment opportunities in the office occupations and have created such white-collar jobs as programmer, systems analyst, auxiliary equipment operator, console operator, tape librarian, word processing proofreader, word processing center coordinator, manager of word processing and administrative secretarial services, proofreader-trainer, scheduler or logger, word processing specialist, professional secretarial supervisor, correspondence secretary, and administrative support secretary.

Business organization now requires a flow of information on an almost instantaneous basis. To cope with this need, business invested in automated data processing equipment. Recognizing the power of this equipment to give fast, accurate, and detailed data on which to base decisions, management continued to add new applications. Thus, clerical staffs grew and are continuing to increase to handle the data that is fed into the systems and that is retrieved. However, a greater premium will be placed on the speed and accuracy of the workers who handle the information.

Business is also investing in word processing centers to reduce costs and to increase office efficiency and productivity. This reorganization of the traditional secretarial job requires a more specialized clerical worker, a word processor whose output is subjected to work standards and work measurements.

The more boring and tedious types of paperwork will be taken care of by machines, freeing human manpower for more interesting and creative work. The office jobs of the future will be more challenging, require greater skill, be more varied, and undoubtedly provide increased opportunities for promotion.

Skills such as typewriting, shorthand, and filing will still be in great demand, and general abilities such as a good command of

English and an understanding of the principles of economics will also be of great importance. Upgraded jobs will require higher degrees of skill and accuracy on the part of the employees.

A good foundation in the skill subjects will enable the office worker to be flexible, since it is expected that in the coming years, the average worker will change jobs several times in a lifetime. Flexibility is the key to success in an automated world. Not all the necessary training will be given in the schools, but a knowledge of basic principles will make on-the-job training relatively simple. More and more schools are today beginning to acquire automated equipment for training students.

It must be remembered, too, that not all offices have purchased automated equipment. Data processing today is a huge industry in itself. Smaller users have access to computers which are used on a time-sharing basis. (A company may own or rent its own computers; it may buy the use of time on somebody else's computer; or it may take its data processing work to a service center for processing.) Generally, these firms hire their own programmers who enter the data in leased computers. Still other companies have a smaller volume of work and find it more economical to continue to work by hand. There are still many opportunities for employment in such places. In other organizations, although word processing centers are developing rapidly, only 15 percent of the offices have word processing installations, and the traditional secretary will continue to be in demand in the foreseeable future.

AUTOMATED COMMUNICATION
OF NUMBERS AND WORDS

Data communications, a term widely used in the modern office, is the movement of business information or data from one person or place to another by electronic equipment. Most data communications make use of long distance telephone lines and terminal equipment such as typewriters and magnetic tape.

This new process gives rise to a need for skilled clerks. Such a system accepts information at the point it is generated, moves it to the point of processing (computer), and then sends it to the point of use. For example, an airline reservation clerk at a remote point keys in a seat reservation to a central computer; while the customer is waiting, the clerk gets instantaneous confirmation in return. In another application, a branch office of an insurance company sends instructions about a claimant's policy to a computer at the main office that is 2,000 miles away. In these new communication services, the operator can also use a dial telephone to transmit and receive data by electronic means.

The clerk, like other office personnel, processes and communicates business information. The data transmitted eventually terminate in the hands of a person who will use the information; therefore, trained personnel are necessary to plan, organize, develop, and utilize such a system effectively. People, as well as machines, are vital in this communication process so that information that is processed by the computer can be "moved" to the proper place at a designated time and in the proper form. Clerical workers are essential in controlling the office function and must be skilled in handling the input and output of such systems.

In organizations with word processing centers, the flow of information begins with the word originator, who is typically the executive. This individual dictates reports, letters, or statistical information onto tapes, belts, or cassettes through an ordinary telephone code or through a more sophisticated telephone system; a central recorder in the word processing center picks up the information, and office personnel use text-editing typewriters to convert these communications into typewritten pages. Word processing systems may extend outside the firm to include the linking of dictation units and automatic typewriters at locations around the country, the use of facsimile equipment to send documents over ordinary phone lines, and electronic input to computerized data banks. Word processing specialists are needed to operate the system from origin of communication to print-out, storage, and retrieval.

PROJECTIONS FOR 1985

Clerical workers are the largest single category in white-collar employment, and employment growth for certain types of clerical workers will be affected by technological developments. For example, a projection of the economy in 1985 by the U.S. Bureau of Labor Statistics indicates that there will be a reduction of clerical workers employed in some routine jobs, such as filing, sorting bank checks, making up payroll, keeping inventory controls, and billing customers because of the use of electronic computers, bookkeeping machines, and other mechanical devices to process routine and repetitive work. However, there will be a demand for clerical personnel to prepare computer inputs. The rapid rise in the word processing market which utilizes central dictation systems and automatic electronic typewriters will require secretarial specialists, both word processors and administrative support secretaries, to operate the equipment. Future predictions of office systems anticipate the likely convergence of electronic data processing and word processing into an integrated office system that will require employees who can think words as well as numbers.

A major factor in the projected level of clerical demand is the rapid growth of service industries (not manufacturing), such as finance, insurance, and real estate, that employ large clerical staffs. Employment in these areas rose from 3.7 million in 1968 to 4.1 million in 1974 and by 1980, will reach 4.6 million. There will also be many new jobs in wholesale and retail trade establishments, in manufacturing firms, and in government agencies.

The chart below indicates the projected rate of growth from 1972 to 1985 for some clerical jobs:

CHART 3
Projected Rate Of Growth For Clerical Jobs*
1972-1985

Job Title	Estimated Employment 1972	Projected Requirements 1985	Percent Growth 1972-1985
Cashiers	998,000	1,360,000	36.1
File Clerks	272,000	318,000	16.7
Office Machine Operators	195,000	230,000	17.9
Receptionists	436,000	650,000	50.0
Statistical Clerks	299,000	375,000	25.8
Stock Clerks	511,000	750,000	46.2
Typists	1,021,000	1,400,000	38.7

*Based on Bureau of Labor Statistics (Bulletin 1824, 1974)

The reasons for the high demand for skilled office workers are basic: the office worker is needed in every community, large or small, and in every type of activity; the population is growing; more information from more sources is being collected from more places; the government is requiring greater reporting; more complex business operations require more data inputs for decision making; and more diversification within companies requires more data compilations and more communications with branches in other sections of the country.

All evidence points to the fact that there is an increasing demand for persons who are familiar with and who are trained in automatic data and word processing. There are also many job opportunities for young people who have good skills, are adaptable, and are anxious to accept positions of high responsibility in automated offices.

THE MINORITIES AND DISADVANTAGED

Many programs in private industry and in government have helped overcome barriers to employment for great numbers of minorities and disadvantaged workers. There also is pressure on business to hire disadvantaged youth. Through training and retraining programs, the federal government has made it possible for those who are unemployed or on the fringes of the labor force to become permanent, full-time workers. It has helped train those employed in low-income jobs to become more productive and successful, and it has discovered and will continue to ascertain the potential of those now considered unemployable.

Programs authorized by the Manpower Development and Training Act (MDTA) of 1962, the Economic Opportunity Act in 1964, and subsequent legislation—Job Opportunities in the Business Sector (JOBS), Neighborhood Youth Corps, Public Service Careers (PSC), Work Incentive Program (WIN), MDTA Institutional Training, Operation Mainstream, Jobs for Progress (SER), and Urban League on-the-job training—have been successful in promoting productive employment of jobless and under-employed youths and adults. The Acts have provided opportunities and money for training. It is interesting that 41 percent of the trainees of the Manpower Development and Training Act are being prepared for clerical and sales jobs, showing that there is a vital need in this area.

The Comprehensive Employment and Training Act of 1973 (CETA), a more recent law, provides for a decentralized system of federal, state, and local manpower activities that include basic education, skills training in the classroom or on the job, supportive services such as child care and transportation, testing, and counseling. Under this Act, most federal and manpower training funds are distributed to the state and local governments directly based on need.

To alleviate the obstacles Vietnam-era veterans encountered in securing and holding jobs, the federal government passed the

President's Veterans Program (PVP) in 1971; PVP then was amended by the Vietnam-Era Veterans Readjustment Assistance Act of 1972. As part of a six-point program to expand occupational training and placement opportunities, the Secretary of Labor was mandated to work with the National Alliance of Businessmen (NAB) in creating job opportunities in private industry. A 57 percent increase in employment for this group occurred between 1972 and 1974, a significant increase when compared to less than 10 percent for the economy as a whole.

Further information on federally aided training programs can be obtained from the local office of your state employment service.

Mr. Robert W. Stein, former manager of Employee Development for the Fisher Scientific Company in Pittsburgh, Pennsylvania, says with authority, in view of his experience as a training and development specialist with several major companies, that the disadvantaged young woman or man considering clerical employment should do so optimistically, for:

"Applicants who can demonstrate that they have something to offer, something that will help in the achievement of organizational goals, will be interviewed and appraised more honestly now than ever before. This means that the individual comtemplating clerical employment must make certain that he or she enters the job market with the proper skills, knowledge, and attitude not only to acquire a desirable position but to do well in this position once it has been secured. To the aspiring young person, I would just like to say: Prepare yourself in these three areas, and I think you will find the road to success much less rocky than you anticipated."

CHANGES IN AGE AND SEX OF CLERICAL WORKERS

It is no surprise that women are becoming a greater part of the

CHART 4

**Increase in
Women Workers in
Total Labor Force
1920-1976**

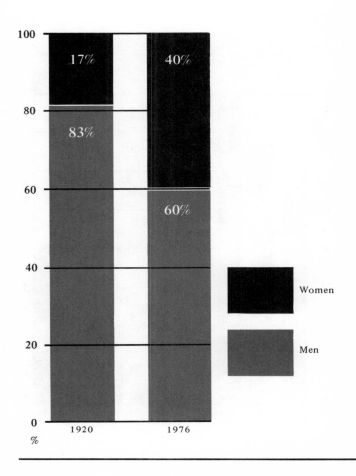

CHART 5

**Increase in Number of Men and Women
Employed in Labor Force**
1950-1973*

*based on data from
U.S. Department of Labor

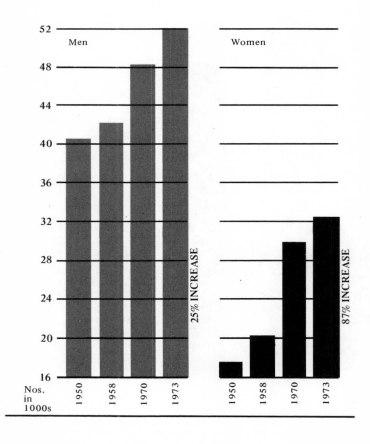

labor force. In 1920, in all occupations there were two women workers for every ten men workers; today, nearly four out of every ten American workers are women. (See Chart 4.) Statistics indicate that from 1950-1973, the increase in the number of women workers exceeded the increase in the number of men. The number of employed women rose from 17.3 million to 32.4 million, a jump of 87 percent compared to a 25 percent rise for men, from 41.6 million to 52.0 million. (See Chart 5.) Forty-nine percent of all women between the ages of eighteen and sixty-four were working, and nine out of ten women will work outside the home at some time during their lives.*

Within the clerical occupations are certain categories that employ larger percentages of women than others. The chart below, based on figures from the Bureau of Labor Statistics, indicates which clerical occupations employ the most women:

CHART 6
Clerical Occupations In Which Three-Fourths
Or More Of The Workers Are Women, 1974

Occupations with over nine-tenths women:	*Percent*
Keypunch Operators	90
Receptionists	97
Secretaries	99.2
Stenographers	95
Telephone Operators	93.8
Tellers	91.5
Typists	96.2
Occupations with over four-fifths women:	
Bookkeepers	89.2
Cashiers	87.7
File Clerks	85
Occupations with about three-fourths women:	
Office Machine Operators	75.3
Payroll Clerks	77

*The Myth and the Reality, U.S. Department of Labor, Women's Bureau (Washington, D.C.: May, 1974).

It is not too surprising to find women in over nine-tenths of the telephone operator or secretarial positions, but it is quite surprising to discover that even the bookkeeping positions, which have been traditionally held by men, are now more than four-fifths filled by women.

There remain, however, a few clerical positions in which men still predominate, as the following chart shows.

CHART 7

Clerical Occupations In Which About
Three-Fourths Or More Of The Workers Are Men, 1974

	Percent
Dispatchers and Starters	75.8
Express Messengers and Railway Mail Clerks	76.3
Mail Carriers	92.5
Messengers	81.0
Postal Clerks	77.4
Programmers	75.0
Shipping and Receiving Clerks	84.1
Stock Clerks	75.0
Systems Analysts	90.0

The findings of the Bangs and Hillestad study* on automated data processing indicated that, in 1968, men also predominated in the following relatively newer office jobs: unit record equipment operators, 63 percent; computer console operator, 90 percent; programmer, 82 percent; data processing manager, 93 percent; and systems analyst, 92 percent. However, 98 percent of the keypunch operators and 65 percent of the tape librarians were women. This last statistic differs from that of 1974 Department of Labor figures which showed that women held 90 percent of the keypunch operator and 45 percent of the console and auxiliary equipment operator jobs, from the total figure of 500,000 persons employed as console, auxiliary equipment, and keypunch operators.

---

*F. Kendrick Bangs and Mildred C. Hillestad, *Automated Data Processing for Education,* Management Information Services, Detroit, Michigan, 1968.

One more look at statistics indicates a "new mix" of working women—a group of married, divorced, separated, or single women, and some well along in age (over 55 years). Of the nearly 35 million women in the labor force in 1973, 42 percent of them were married and working, and 40 percent had children under the age of 18. In March, 1975, working wives comprised 44.4 percent of the labor force, 72 percent of whom were working full-time. In April, 1976, of the 86½ million persons employed in the work force, nearly 35 million were women, of whom 35.3 percent were clerical workers.

Young women today do not enter the work force with the intention of staying only until they marry. They often continue in their positions for many years, and large numbers of married women start their careers late in life. Approximately half of the 35 million working women work to support themselves or to help raise their families' standard of living.

Just what is the significance of all these statistics? Even to the high school student not yet at work, they have meaning. In general, they say:

1. That there are now and probably will continue to be proportionately more jobs in the clerical field than in others.

2. That most clerical occupations are feminized, except for some key positions in data processing and office management.

3. That the automation of processes in business and industry, accompanied by the growing complexity of business and industry, has increased the need for clerical workers.

4. That additional training will be needed to fill the new jobs brought about by automation.

5. That, as statistics indicate that work is today not merely a stop gap until marriage, management will give more

consideration to additional training for women and there will be increasingly more opportunities for them to advance to higher positions.

6. That education becomes more important as it becomes apparent that today's training will be used for many years.

7. That legislation enacted during the past decade barring discrimination in employment on the basis of sex should make available new opportunities for women, should enable them to secure more diversified jobs, and should enable women to secure and advance to jobs requiring more responsibility and a higher skill level than was formerly possible.

CLASSIFICATIONS OF WORKERS
IN THE CLERICAL OCCUPATIONS

People who process papers in offices or handle related activities are classed as *clerical workers.* Depending on their duties, there are many kinds of clerical workers: general clerks, special clerks (such as mail, payroll, or file clerks), machine operators, bookkeepers, stenographers, secretaries, proofreaders, and copy editors. In a small office, there may be only one general office worker who does all of the paperwork connected with the operation. One employer will call this worker "my clerk"; another will refer to the employee as "my secretary"; and a third may call this same person "my assistant."

In larger offices, the duties become more specialized, and office management has been trying for years to develop specific titles that have specific meaning so that everybody can understand what is meant by a job title. Job classification, though, is in its infancy; and a person has only to read the "Help Wanted" column to realize that one company may advertise for a "secretary" while another company will describe identical duties and ask for a "clerk."

The definitions of titles used in this book are taken from the government's attempt at standardization, *The Dictionary of Occupational Titles.* * According to this source, a general clerk (office clerk routine) performs any combination of the following and similar clerical tasks not requiring knowledge of systems or procedures:

> Writes or types bills, statements, receipts, checks, or other documents, copying information from one record to another. Proofreads records or forms. Counts, weighs or measures material. Sorts and files records. Receives money from customers and deposits money in bank. Addresses envelopes or packages by hand or with typewriter or addressograph machine. Stuffs envelopes by hand or with envelope stuffing machine. Answers telephone, conveys messages, and runs errands. Stamps, sorts, and distributes mail. Stamps or numbers forms by hand or machine. Operates office duplicating equipment.

A general office clerk (administrative clerk) performs a variety of the following or similar clerical duties, utilizing knowledge of systems or procedures:

> Copies data and compiles records and reports. Tabulates and posts data in record books. Computes wages, taxes, premiums, commissions, and payments. Records orders for merchandise or service. Gives

---

*The Dictionary of Occupational Titles, Vols. I and II (Washington: U.S. Government Printing Office, 1965).

information to and interviews customers, claimants, employees, and sales personnel. Receives, counts, and pays out cash. Prepares, issues, and sends out receipts, bills, policies, invoices, statements, and checks. Prepares stock inventory. Adjusts complaints. Operates office machines, such as typewriter, adding, calculating, and duplicating machines. Opens and routes incoming mail. May take dictation. May prepare payroll. May keep books. May purchase supplies. May be designated according to field of activity as Death-Claim Clerk (insurance); or according to location of employment as Airport Clerk (air transportation); Camp Clerk; Colliery Clerk (mining and quarrying).

In addition to general clerks with nonspecialized duties, there are highly specialized types of clerks who perform one routine duty at a high level of competency. For instance, a person who runs off mimeograph stencils all day long is classified as a duplicating machine clerk. A clerk whose sole duty is to compute payrolls on the comptometer or National Cash Register Accounting Machine is a payroll clerk. For practical purposes, the term *clerk* refers to one who performs office duties not generally assigned to bookkeepers, stenographers, salespeople, or managers.

Office positions are classified on different levels, depending on such factors as the educational requirements, amount of supervision required, amount of responsibility assumed, special skills required, or risk involved.

The Administrative Management Society has prepared a condensed guide for 20 job classifications that gives a quick overall picture of common types of clerical positions in offices throughout the United States and Canada.

JOB TITLES AND DESCRIPTIONS*

1. MAIL CLERK–FILE CLERK

   Circulates office mail; delivers messages and supplies. May process incoming or outgoing mail, operate related machines, and perform other routine duties. Performs routine filing and sorting operations according to an established system; locates and removes material upon request and keeps records of its disposition. May perform related clerical duties.

2. GENERAL CLERK B

   Performs clerical duties in accordance with established procedures. Maintains records and may prepare reports from basic data which do not require the development of secondary data. Job requires considerable supervision.

3. GENERAL CLERK A

   Performs complex and responsible clerical duties requiring independent analysis, exercise of judgment, and a detailed knowledge of department or company policies and procedures. Minimum supervision required.

4. ACCOUNTING CLERK B

   Checks, verifies, and posts journal vouchers, accounts payable vouchers, or other simple accounting data of a recurring or standard nature.

5. ACCOUNTING CLERK A

   Keeps a complete set of accounting records in a small office or handles one phase of accounting in a larger unit which requires the accounting training needed to determine proper accounting entries, prepares account-

----

Office Salaries Survey, 1975, Administrative Management Society.

ing reports, analyzes accounting records to determine causes of results shown, etc. May direct work of junior clerks or bookkeepers. (Excludes supervisors.)

6. BOOKKEEPING MACHINE OPERATOR
Operates a bookkeeping machine to record business transactions of a recurring and standardized nature, where proper posting has been indicated or is readily identifiable. May balance to control figures.

7. OFFSET DUPLICATING MACHINE OPERATOR
Sets up and operates offset duplicating machines. Cleans and adjusts equipment but does not make repairs. May prepare own plates and operate auxiliary equipment and may keep records of kind and amount of work done.

8. TELEPHONE SWITCHBOARD OPERATOR
Operates a single or multiple position PBX telephone switchboard. May keep records of calls and toll charges, operate a paging system, and perform duties of receptionist.

9. TYPIST—CLERK
Types letters, reports, tabulations, and other material in which set-ups and terms are generally clear and follow a standard pattern. May prepare stencils or offset masters. Performs clerical duties of moderate difficulty.

10. STENOGRAPHER
Transcribes from dictating equipment or records and transcribes shorthand dictation involving a normal range of business vocabulary. May perform copy typing or clerical work of moderate difficulty incidental to primary stenographic duties. May operate as a member of a centralized stenographic area. May perform the secretarial function for a small group.

11. SECRETARY B

Performs secretarial duties for a member of middle management. General requirements are the same as for Secretary A (listed below), but limited to the area of responsibility of the principal.

12. SECRETARY A

Performs secretarial duties for a top-level executive or a person responsible for a major function or geographic operation. Does work of a confidential nature and relieves principal of designated administrative details. Requires initiative, judgment, knowledge of company practices, policy, and organization.

13. CORRESPONDENCE SECRETARY

Operates all types of automated equipment in a word processing center and is responsible for transcribing and copy typing the many types of work handled in the center.

14. KEYPUNCH OPERATOR B

Operates an alphabetical or numerical keypunch machine to record pre-coded or readily usable data following generally standardized procedures. May verify the work of others, using a verifying machine.

15. KEYPUNCH OPERATOR A

Operates an alphabetical or numerical keypunch machine or verifier to record or verify complex or uncoded data, working from source material which may not be arranged for keypunching. Selects appropriate number and kinds of cards. Follows a pattern of operations generally standardized but frequently including rules, exceptions, and special instructions which demand operator's close attention.

16. TABULATING MACHINE OPERATOR

Sets up, operates, and wires a variety of punched card equipment, including tabulators and multipliers. Wires boards from diagrams prepared by others for routine jobs or uses prewired boards on complex or repetitive jobs. May locate and correct job difficulties and assist in training less experienced operators.

17. COMPUTER OPERATOR B

Operates computers utilizing established programs or programs under development. Loads computer and manipulates control switch on console in accordance with programmed instructions. Observes functioning of equipment. Detects nature of errors or equipment failure and makes normal console adjustments. Maintains necessary operating records.

18. COMPUTER OPERATOR A

Operates computer utilizing established programs or programs under development. Oversees loading of computer and manipulation of controls. Detects nature of errors or equipment failure. May instruct or give limited directions to less experienced operators.

19. PROGRAMMER

With general supervision, analyzes and defines programs for electronic data processing equipment. Is generally competent in most phases of programming to work on his own and requires only general guidance for the balance of the activities. Conducts analyses of sufficient detail of all defined systems specifications and develops block diagrams and machine logic flow charts; codes and prepares test data; tests and debugs programs. Revises and refines programs as required and documents all procedures used throughout the computer program when it is formally established. Evaluates and modifies existing programs to take into account changes in systems requirements. May give technical assistance to lower level classifications. Normally progresses from this classification to a Lead Programmer.

20. SYSTEMS ANALYST

Under close supervision, assists in devising computer system specifications and record layouts. Is qualified to work on several phases of systems analysis but requires guidance and direction for other phases. Conducts studies and analyses of existing and proposed operations. Prepares all levels of computer block diagram and may assist in the preparation of machine logic flow charting.

Akademie van Wetenschappen, Amsterdam. Afdeeling voor
de Wis-en Natuurkundige Wetenschappen. Proceedings.
Series C. Biological and Medical Sciences. Amsterdam.

[Formerly as: Nederlandse Akademie van Wetenschappen.
        Proceedings. Series C. Biological and
        Medical Sciences.]

Chapter 2

THE CLERK

Every business organization requires clerks to perform basic office functions. The clerk's duties vary depending on his position. A glance at the help-wanted ads of any local newspaper will indicate the need for clerks in all categories, such as mail clerk, stock clerk, telephone switchboard clerk, telephone order clerk, personnel clerk, file clerk, and receptionist clerk. There are more clerks in business occupations than in any other category of worker below the management level.

Clerical work carries the lowest classification among the office positions. It ranks lowest in the salary scale, and it requires less specialized job preparation than any other office position. On the other hand, it is the most common job for which the beginning worker is hired, and it is often used as the job station in which a new employee learns the work of the office. Although office technology has created new job opportunities, it is important to realize that jobs are declining for those who have limited training and who are able to perform only simple, routine tasks. Basic to job success in most clerical positions is a knowledge of typing, business English, office practices, and human relations skills. Equally important are good attitudes: cooperativeness, dependability, promptness, accuracy, honesty, and responsibility.

A few years ago, the usual practice in business was to hire superior academically prepared graduates for clerical work and train them on the job. This procedure, however, cost the employer too much money, for the employees often found that, after trying it at company expense, they were not suited to routine work and soon resigned. Business today is more likely to look to the high schools for its clerks, who have been trained at public expense. These clerically trained graduates become productive workers much sooner, do not object to the routine work involved, and are willing to stay on their jobs.

Most of the large firms in the United States provide some type of on-the-job training or orientation programs for their new employees and retraining for the relocation of their older employees. Progressive companies recognize that training on the job leads to work satisfaction and personal fulfillment, thus making an employee more valuable.

Though clerical work is often rather routine, there are varied types of clerical jobs which may appeal to different interests and abilities. In addition to general clerks, who may perform tasks of a varying nature, there are such specialized clerks as file clerks, clerk typists, receptionist-clerks, data typists, and tape perforator operators. The jobs at the bottom of the skill ladder are diminishing, and there is an increasing need for specialization because of automation in the office.

CHANGING ACTIVITIES OF THE CLERK

The modern office functions as the nerve center of management, which is the brain of the business organization. This nerve center, which is composed of clerical workers, must function with accuracy and speed.

Many of the detailed and repetitive tasks have been automated, and the work performed is more sophisticated than it was.

Some of the responsibilities of the clerk today are:

Opening mail
Handling the telephone
Handling and sorting source documents, such as requisitions,
    bills, payment checks, notices, and adjustments
Filling in printed forms on the typewriter

Copying from rough draft or corrected copy on the typewriter

Receiving callers

Cataloging addresses, prices, and other data

Typing numeric data

Writing numeric data

Proofreading numeric data

Duplicating or copying information (Xerox and offset machines)

Using the calculating machine, particularly the 10-key electronic calculator

Detecting errors

Handling printed reports, the output

Recording data in handwritten form

Keying-in data into typewriters, cash registers, calculators,
keypunch machines, and key-to-tape machines to get
printouts

Verifying or listing information about business papers

Coding information

Readying data to be converted to machine-reading language

Microfilming

Using indexing systems for mechanized storage

Retrieving data from microfilm, magnetic tapes, and documents

Composing and typing letters

Reviewing machine outputs

Amending corrected data and entering it properly into the
system

Performing research

The ability to operate other office machines and to file
business papers usually is required, too.

According to one study*, most of the basic tasks performed
by office workers involve working with figures. (See below
for other data.)

---

*Frank Lanham and others, *Development of Performance Goals for a
New Office and Business Education Learnings System.* Columbus: The
Center for Vocational and Technical Education, 1970.

Functional Area	Number of Basic Tasks Included
1. Numerical clerical records (Includes not only tasks requiring knowledge of bookkeeping and/or accounting but also computation or checking of numerical data)	969
2. Internal services (Includes mailing, filing, duplicating, recording of a non-computational type)	750
3. Typing communication (Includes only tasks not included in other categories. Typewriting is performed in all functional departments. Includes typewriting and stenographic pools)	644
4. Client-related services (Includes only service-related offices as contrasted with sales in a product-related office)	437
5. Oral communication	425
6. Electronic data processing (Does not include preparing material for input or working with printouts)	398
7. Personnel	338
8. Sales	230
9. Shipping, receiving, inventory	134
10. Purchasing	85
11. Production	40
12. Miscellaneous	

WHAT SKILLS ARE IMPORTANT?

Clerical workers are no longer just cogs in the wheels; rather, the jobs they perform are pertinent to the overall goals of businesses. They must, therefore, be aware of the total business operation and must assume a sense of responsibility in their work. Concomitant with this obligation are good attitudes and the necessity for promptness, for accuracy, for meeting deadlines, for follow-up, for initiative, and for wise judgment.

Clerical workers also must be skilled in listening to and carrying out instructions, reading, handwriting, arithmetic, and writing (grammatical sentence construction, spelling, and punctuation). They also must have the ability to communicate orally via the telephone and in person-to-person contact; and, equally important, they must be able to get along with people, both inside and outside the company. Good clerical workers must also be able to accept and act upon valid criticism.

Every clerical job involves typewriting, and the typist's job itself has become more sophisticated, requiring more background in business and more independent judgment. Additionally, those who aspire to clerical positions should be able to operate numerous other office machines and file business papers. Considerable effort has been made to establish standards of performance in the commonest clerical jobs. In general, it can be said that a clerk should be able to:

- Type at least 55 words per minute.
- File cards or remove them from the files at the rate of 300 per hour.
- Cut a mimeograph stencil in 20 minutes.
- Fill in 100-150 addresses on form letters by typewriter in an hour.

A recent study of 204 business firms revealed that good spelling and typewriting skills and a good attitude were important qualifications for beginning secretarial and clerical employees.* According to the results of the study, the following skills and attributes (in order of importance) were considered essential by the firms surveyed:

---

*Leonard Robertson, "Office Requirements in the Portland Standard Metropolitan Area," *The Delta Pi Epsilon Journal,* Vol. XVIII, No. 1, November, 1975, p. 15.

SKILLS

Spelling ability
Typewriting proficiency
Operation of automatic typewriter
Operation of calculating machine
Operation of transcribing machine
Ability to take shorthand

ATTRIBUTES

Regular job attendance
Cooperation
Courtesy
Good telephone personality
Good personal appearance

EDUCATIONAL PREPARATION

In most companies, high school graduation is the minimum educational requirement for employment in clerical work. Usually, the employer also wants specialized training for office work; and many high schools have developed clerical curricula to prepare graduates for those office duties not generally assigned to bookkeepers, stenographers, salespeople, or managers. The business subjects usually included, and those which will be vocationally most useful to the clerk, are: typewriting, bookkeeping or recordkeeping, clerical or office practice, introduction to business, and consumer economics.

Students from schools offering only general education components have the option of attending an area vocational school for training. Noteworthy is a unique program offered by the Office Occupations Divisions in the 916 area vocational technical institutes in Minnesota which teaches students the skills required for specialized office employment. The twelve curricula offered in this program qualify graduates as: timekeepers, accounts receivable clerks, records management clerks, policy typists, claims clerks, records clerks, raters, policy analysts and interpreters, expeditors, dispatchers, and tracing clerks. This training prepares students for work in a variety of offices (educational, banking and finance, accounting, traffic, purchasing, law enforcement, insurance, and medical data processing) and is coordinated with the high school districts from which students are transported for two hours of classes each day.

Units of work which usually are included in the clerical practice course are: telephone, duplicating and calculating machines, business filing and records control, personality development, clerical applications of typewriting (filling in forms, making multiple copies, preparing copy for duplicating, or typing from rough draft), basic arithmetic, handwriting, and how to apply for a position. The classes sometimes are organized like real offices to help students learn the interrelationships of different office jobs.

In addition to classroom experiences, students have many other opportunities to learn about office work. One of these is the school business club, which may invite alumni who are business leaders to describe their jobs. The club may sponsor field trips to offices in the neighborhood or arrange other activities to bring business nearer the classroom. Another good learning experience is summer or after-school work in an office. Although the positions for which students who have not yet graduated can qualify will probably involve only routine work, they offer plenty of opportunities to learn about office procedures and how to get along with fellow workers. Another way to get some office experience prior to graduation from high school is to work in your school's office. Sometimes this work is assigned as part of a clerical practice course.

Many high schools have a cooperative work-study program. Students go to school half-time and work in offices for pay the other half. They may go to school in the morning and work in the afternoon or go to school and to the office in alternate weeks. A coordinator from the high school supervises the office work and arranges for school training in areas in which the student is deficient.

COMMUNITY COLLEGES

Although clerical workers in past decades usually were trained in high schools, the community college, which had its greatest impetus in vocational education offerings during the 1960s and 1970s, has taken over part of the high school function—namely, career training designed to prepare students for specific occupations. Typical business programs offered at the community college level are accounting, word processing, marketing and management, records management, secretarial studies, and data processing.

In 1972, the enrollment in community college vocational programs increased by 47 percent, with the secretarial and clerical specialization leading the list of vocational course offerings. Data from a study of The Office of Education for the year ending June, 1971, indicated that approximately half of the 307,880 associate degrees awarded to junior and community college students were in curricula designed to provide occupational competence at the technical or semiprofessional level. Of this figure, 5,017 degrees were granted in "general data processing technologies."*

To bridge the gap between school and work, a supervised, credit-bearing cooperative education internship program is offered in many community colleges. Classroom experience is combined with on-the-job paid employment in students' own fields of study. Frequently, students are offered permanent positions with their internship employers upon graduation.

Occupational Manpower and Training Needs, U.S. Office of Education, Bulletin #1824 (Washington, D.C.: 1974).

Private business schools are also developing cooperative programs, especially for such specialized clerks as keypunch operators. Additionally, some businesses are sending their untrained clerks to private business schools for supplementary training on a part-time basis during their working hours.

COMPANY TRAINING

Business itself provides three basic types of educational programs:

- *On-the-job training* wherein the beginning worker is trained at his assigned job under the supervision of an experienced worker, often assisted by company manuals.

- *Vestibule training* (usually conducted by larger firms) that is given away from the work area but during working hours, usually in an on-site classroom, using the same equipment, materials, and procedures as the actual job. (This training hopefully will raise the employee's level of skill, will orient him to company procedures, and will teach new skills to old employees, enabling them to qualify for promotion.)

- *After-hours or off-premises training,* a volunteer program to improve skills to qualify for promotion, or to improve personal development.

The Metropolitan Life Insurance Company sponsors the Employment Qualifications Program to qualify employees for regular positions as general clerks, typists, or keypunch operators. In this program, three to five hours a day are spent on an assigned job, and two and a half hours a day are spent in improving basic skills.

Consolidated Edison employs workers on an "on-trial" basis for three months, after which they become regular employees, provided their work performance and attendance records are satisfactory. American Airlines has a program to introduce new employees to procedures and forms. The New York Telephone Company trains inexperienced personnel for jobs as clerks, typists, and operators. The McGraw-Hill Book Company, Inc. places its new employees in a training program for three weeks before assigning them to a job. The Eastman-Kodak Company's (Rochester, New York) education programs provide more than 200 courses for Kodak personnel who want to improve their job and communication skills. Instruction ranges from the fundamentals of reading and writing to computer programming.

Office equipment companies often find that there is an inadequate supply of operators for their machines. They know, too, that their customers will buy equipment only if the operators produce more work on it. Because it is to their interest to have competent operators, they maintain company training schools.

OTHER TRAINING PROGRAMS

As already mentioned in Chapter 1, training for clerical jobs also has been made possible through federally subsidized programs. Approximately 65,000 persons completed on-the-job training projects during 1969; 82 percent of these subsequently were employed in the jobs for which they had received training. Of the 40,000 persons who completed Manpower Development and Training Act (MDTA) programs in 1973 and who found jobs in their fields, 6,500 were in office occupations. A summary of the effectiveness of one MDTA clerk-stenographer training center in the Appalachia area revealed that graduates of the program had been elevated to high levels of productivity, 62 percent had found employment in the occupation for which they had been trained, and 20 percent had found employment in related occupations. Completion of the program resulted in better jobs and higher salaries, and the ratings for the potential success of the trainees were high.*

Another unique plan for bridging the gap between school and work was innovated by representatives of Columbia University, The Ford Foundation, and the National Commission for Manpower Policy. In this program, vouchers are used to subsidize employers for hiring and training particular workers.

ABILITIES REQUIRED IN TOMORROW'S OFFICES

Office procedures are affected by technological advances. The office worker who advances beyond his entry-level job and who is involved in the processing of data needs an overall understanding of how a business operates. He must be able to respond to the new methods of collecting, processing, storing, and retrieving information.

Huffman and Gust** asked office managers what will be required in tomorrow's office. The abilities necessary now and in the future by clerical workers are:

1. Ability to perceive the total communication system of an organization as a vast network of information flow.
2. Ability to adjust quickly to new equipment, procedures, and work sequences brought about by rapid technological changes for the purpose of updating skills and increasing individual productive capacity.

---

*John J. Stallard, "A Model for the Evaluation of the MTDA Skill Center Clerk-Stenographer Program," *The Delta Pi Epsilon Journal,* Vol. XVII, No. 2, February, 1975, pp. 34-37.

**Harry Huffman and Dale D. Gust, *Business Education for the Emergent Office,* The Center for Vocational and Technical Education, The Ohio State University, June, 1970.

3. Ability to adapt to different systems. (Total job flexibility.)

4. Ability to recognize how inaccurate data entering a system may affect outcomes on succeeding jobs.

5. Ability to gain rapport with all racial groups.

6. Ability to communicate via data communication devices and to know the limitations, methods of utilization, and capacity of equipment to perform particular operations.

7. Ability to input data in an on-line, real-time system to obtain information for report preparation, office work production, and exception reporting.

8. Ability to review information systems output to determine if there are errors.

9. Ability to determine what happened to produce the results in an information system and to provide corrections of data, if needed.

10. Ability to utilize such contemporary record storage techniques as microfilm, microfiche, aperture cards, etc., including indexing and operating the system.

11. Ability to operate various pieces of new equipment through self-instruction or in-service training. (MT/ST, electronic calculator, ATS, etc.)

12. Ability to operate various computer data manipulation devices.

13. Ability to operate microfilm and microfiche equipment.

14. Ability to convert data to appropriate coding schemes.

15. Ability to assemble and arrange input data for processing.

Perhaps this list exaggerates the requirements for an initial job, but it certainly indicates the directions the worker must take for promotion.

HOW TO GET STARTED

Business often seeks office employees through school place-ment offices. That is one reason why good personality ratings in school and the attainment of high grades and specific skills are important. Too often, graduates by-pass the placement office and try to get their jobs unaided, despite the fact that the office is there to assist them. Get acquainted with your placement office director whose job it is to help graduates by matching job openings with qualified candidates. It is your responsibility to complete the necessary forms for registration and report to the office regularly.

Information about job leads may come through friends or relatives. Many companies regard their present employees as their best recruiters of new workers. To follow such a lead is an accepted practice, but it is only the initial contact. From there on, the qualifications of the applicants usually decide whether they get the job.

An excellent job can sometimes be obtained by applying at a private employment agency. The agency will have job candidates fill out application forms and, after assessing their skills, may send them on several interviews. Many companies like to hire people directly from employment agencies, since the agencies first "screen" all applicants and send only those who seem to fit the qualifications. A disadvantage is the fact that a private employment agency charges a fee for its services, usually about a week's salary. However, it is becoming a common practice for the employer to pay the fee.

Many people prefer to use the facilities of the local office of the state employment service. Representatives of these offices very often visit high schools near graduation to explain to the seniors how to register for a position. The location of the state employment service office is easily determined through the local telephone directory; its services are entirely free. In New York State, for example, joint programs are conducted with more than

700 high schools to provide counseling, aptitude testing, and placement for seniors about to enter the labor market. The service is anxious to help employers find qualified workers and to help workers find the most advantageous jobs for which they qualify.

Positions for clerks are listed in the classified section of the newspaper. There are two kinds of want-ads—blind advertisements requiring a letter of application and complete advertisements giving information that enables the applicant to arrange a personal interview at once. A blind advertisement describes the position but does not identify the employing company. The applicant must address a letter of application to a box number; if the letter is successful, the candidate gets the interview. In the recommended reading list at the end of this book, you will find excellent sources of information about how to write letters of application. You should study these carefully before preparing your own application letter.

Because matching people with the right jobs is so important, companies have central personnel departments where all applicants for positions are screened by trained interviewers. Candidates go to the personnel office for their first interviews and usually have conversations with members of the department who form general impressions of applicants' personal appearance, grooming, speech, and poise. The discussions, which usually revolve around candidates' interests and training, give the applicants an opportunity to demonstrate their understanding of the job requirements and to indicate how their qualifications meet those requirements.

Applicants are asked to complete application forms. Since much of clerical work involves instructions, applicants should be most careful to complete the forms exactly as they are told. If the last name should be written first, an application from *Mary Whyte* instead of *Whyte, Mary* will get little attention.

The interview often is followed by a clerical test or a battery of tests which examines for a number of clerical abilities: filing, arithmetic reasoning, spelling, and grammar. Another widely used clerical test involves recognition of similarity or dissimilarity of figures or names. For instance, the testee is asked to check only the names or numbers that are alike in a list such as:

1240459 — 1240459

2220459 — 2202459

John Anderson — John Andersen

Louis Rodriguez — Louis Rodriguez

Applicants for positions as clerks may also be asked to take a test in typewriting. The usual straight-copy test is most often used, but the test may also include typewriting applications, such as preparing a form letter from information given out of context or arranging material properly on the page.

Superior students may have received a certificate for having successfully taken the National Business Entrance Tests in their schools before graduation. Showing the certificate during an interview will improve the applicant's chances of being hired.

After approval by the personnel department, an applicant usually is sent directly to the department in which the vacancy exists for an interview with the supervisor. During this interview, the supervisor discusses the exact nature of the job and also has an opportunity to decide whether the prospective clerk will fit into that particular office and work well with the other clerks already there.

THE WORKING SITUATION

Many people prefer to enter white-collar jobs in offices rather than seek factory jobs because of the generally good working conditions clerical employees enjoy. Additionally, most office workers get longer vacation periods than do blue-collar employees, and their working hours usually are shorter. In many firms, the work shift for clerical workers is being reduced to a 35-hour, 4-day week. This is especially true in companies that have expensive electronic equipment which must be operated on a 24-hour basis. Reports indicate that employees find this schedule convenient because they have more free time; management likes it because there is less absenteeism and greater productivity.

Office employees of large companies also receive many fringe benefits in addition to salary—benefits ranging from medical and hospital care, insurance, retirement pensions, paid vacations, and free lunches, to the privilege of buying stock in the company at reduced quotations. According to the U.S. Chamber of Commerce, benefits approximated 33 percent of the payroll dollar in 1973.

A clerk's job, involving as it does many diversified duties, usually provides opportunities for development and promotion if the ability is there. These opportunities come through the trained supervision that is usually available and may often be supplemented by additional training at company expense. Clerks may specialize in routines which they like and for which they are well-suited, eventually becoming calculator operators, mimeograph clerks, or file clerks. For a person looking for stability and a position which does not require aggressiveness and heavy responsibility, that of specialized clerk is appealing.

Automation has, no doubt, made some changes in the type of work done by clerical employees, but most experts agree that it has not decreased the number of clerical positions. Clerical workers in many offices are now using electric typewriters that automatically type the final copy from rough draft and make all revisions and corrections. Filing continues to be an important part of a clerk's job, but the materials being filed now include such items as punched tapes and recorded discs instead of the usual papers. The ability of the clerk to work accurately—to read and follow instructions—will become increasingly important. The upgraded clerical jobs which are appearing in automated offices may necessitate increased training and higher native ability for clerical workers.

A clerical job provides more regularity of employment than factory work, which is affected by seasonal variations and by supply and demand. The clerk who performs the designated duties satisfactorily can usually count on stability of employment and regular advancement.

PART-TIME AND TEMPORARY EMPLOYMENT

Another advantage of clerical jobs is that they are available to those who are interested in working only part-time or temporarily. Temporaries no longer are just fill-ins for sick or vacationing employees. Companies now staff themselves for a minimum rather than a maximum work flow and use temporary help for additional tasks as they arise or for once-a-year, large-scale jobs. This flexible staffing also offers advantages in terms of employee recruitment and hiring. The part-timer may be kept on the agency's payroll for a probationary period, after which time a good worker may be hired and transferred to the regular company payroll. Temporary or part-time work offers a decided advantage to the employee, too. If the worker is not suited to the job and performs poorly, a separation does not carry the same stigma of "being fired" as it would for a permanent, full-time employee.

DISADVANTAGES

There are, of course, disadvantages to becoming a clerk. An ambitious person would use the job only as an entering wedge to get into the business world and would do everything possible to progress to a higher level of responsibility as soon as possible. Routine work is monotonous and lacks challenge; and many clerical jobs are just keypunching, reading, and recording data. Only a person unwilling to assume responsibility would want to stay in it for an extended period of time.

Routine clerical jobs are very much like factory piecework in that production standards can be set and output measured. Clerks in a company with high production standards may feel that they are under too much pressure in their jobs and that the standards are unrealistic. If supervision is poor, there may be peak loads of paperwork at the end of the month, for example, which add pressure to the job.

The final disadvantage of being a clerk is salary. Because clerks' jobs have the lowest skill requirements among clerical occupations, they also are the lowest paid. The worker who doesn't eventually achieve a rating above that of clerk will remain among the lowest-paid office workers.

PROMOTION OPPORTUNITIES FOR CLERKS

Promotion opportunities are available to the employee, male or female, who qualifies, demonstrates responsibility, and possesses the ability to handle challenges. Today, capable women are advancing more rapidly than their male counterparts because of the anti-discrimination movements and the Equal Employment Opportunity Act of 1972. However, there still are disproportionate numbers of men in jobs at higher levels while many women are still working at levels below their training or at higher levels under low-paid titles. An increasing number of firms are participating in job restructuring to offer promotional opportunities equally to both men and women.

There are no clear-cut steps up the promotion ladder in business. Some clerks may move into a classification of stenographer, then to secretary. Other clerks may move from their first position into a job as assistant to the supervisor of the clerical pool and, eventually, into the shoes of the supervisor. Still another clerk may enter quite unrelated work after an apprenticeship—selling, for instance.

Automation has opened up new promotional opportunities for clerks. Many clerks can, with training, move from keypunch operator to project director. The most able may be made programmers.

In well managed offices, all employees are rated periodically by their supervisors on such qualities as:

- The ability to learn new methods and techniques.
- Productiveness—the amount of work produced and how promptly it was completed.
- The neatness and accuracy with which work is performed.
- Industriousness—how consistently individuals apply their energies to their daily jobs.
- Initiative—the ability to carry out independently the appointed job and to offer suggestions for improvement.
- Cooperativeness and helpfulness—the ability to act as a team member.
- The knowledge the employee possesses of the job and related duties.

These ratings are discussed with the workers, and opportunities for improvement and for additional training may be given. A clerk who receives superior merit ratings will quickly be cited for advancement.

Most companies have a policy of promotion from within, and one of the functions of the supervisor is preparing workers for the next step upward. Many large companies offer training opportunities within the company. The first in-service courses are usually in skills; the next courses involve semisupervisory or supervisory training; and final courses are offered in the field of management itself. In cases where training inside the company seems uneconomical or impractical, arrangements sometimes are made for workers to take courses in business schools, colleges, or universities outside the company. Assistance is given in various forms— payment for books, transportation, tests, and laboratory fees; partial reimbursement for tuition at time of registration and the balance when the course is completed; full payment to institution directly or partial payment on a sliding scale based on grade earned. In many cases, the employing company pays the full cost of these courses in order to develop employees.

In a recent survey, 90 percent of the 283 respondents from large corporations indicated that their firms had tuition-aid plans to assist in employee development and to be an attractive fringe benefit. The average age of the employee taking advantage of this opportunity was between twenty and thirty-nine.*

Of course, formally organized in-service courses are limited to larger companies, but smaller companies sometimes provide a wider variety of work experiences and closer association with management that compensate for the elaborate training facilities of the big corporations.

TYPES OF MACHINES COMMONLY OPERATED BY CLERKS

Some of the most common office machines operated by clerks are typewriters, voice-writing machines, duplicators, punching, sorting and tabulating machines, and calculators.

Typewriter

Ability to type is basic to most clerical work, but the degree of proficiency required depends on the job at hand. The most

---

*Charles E. Watson and Alexis L. Grzybowski, "What Your Company Should Know About Tuition-Aid Plans," *Business Horizons,* October, 1975, pp. 75-80.

common brands of manual typewriters are Royal, Remington, Underwood, and Smith Corona. However, in most offices, these machines have been replaced almost entirely by electric typewriters. A typist who has become proficient in the use of a manual typewriter can easily transfer to an electric typewriter or to a machine with a special keyboard.

Added to the above list of typewriter manufacturers is IBM, a leader in the field of Selectric typewriters. With experience on this electric typewriter, a novice can learn to operate a Magnetic Tape Selectric Typewriter (MT/ST), a Mag Card II typewriter, a memory typewriter, or a correcting Selectric II typewriter rather quickly. The type on the Mag Card, Magnetic Tape, or Memory typewriter is reproduced electronically, and perfect final copy is turned out at 150 words a minute. Input using these machines can appear simultaneously on a Cathode Ray Tube (CRT) screen and also can be read into a computer through an appropriate terminal. Efficient utilization of these machines has led to new managerial concepts, especially word processing, a discussion of which is found in Chapter 5.

In common use in many firms, too, is the automatic typewriter, a machine whose keys are activated by punched tape rather than manual operation. These machines have been in use since the 1930s for repetitive typing. Today, more sophisticated models are used in word processing centers.

There are many type sizes and styles of typewriters, as well as several hundred different keyboards. There are keyboards for practically every language and for many different professions and businesses, such as keyboards equipped with special symbols for use in the fields of astronomy, telegraphy, air navigation, electricity, medicine, pharmacy, physics, engineering, chemistry, biology, meteorology, and mathematics.

Voice-writing Machines

The originator may use a voice-writing machine for dictation, and the clerk (sometimes called transcriber) may type from the record or cassette. Some machines may be attached to a telephone so that the executive may dictate from another location to a central recording and transcribing point.

Most voice-writing machines record on plastic discs, belts, or cassettes. These recordings are durable and may be mailed to a central transcribing pool or word processing center if the originator is away from the office. For instance, a salesperson may leave a customer and dictate a report from an automobile before the next call. The clerk plays back the records or cassettes on a transcribing unit and types what is heard.

The most commonly used voice-writing machines are manufactured under the names Dictaphone, IBM, Stenocord, Edison Voicewriter, and Lanier.

The magnetic tape cassette is very popular today. The unit is compact, and the recording media can be filed, mailed, transcribed, erased, and reused many times.

Duplicators

Special clerks are often employed to operate the duplicating machines. The principal processes of office duplication are: fluid or spirit, stencil, offset, and photographic. With the direct or liquid process, a carbon-typed page is used as the master copy. The copies are made directly from the master copy as it comes in contact with chemically moistened sheets of paper. An alcoholic fluid is used to dissolve and transfer a minute portion of the dye from the master to the paper.

A. B. Dick, Standard Duplicator, and Ditto are popular fluid duplicators.

The stencil-process duplicator is a commonly used office duplicator. It involves a stencil and an inked drum. The stencil is a thin tissue coated with a substance that resists ink. When the typewriter key strikes the stencil, the wax coating is pushed aside, exposing the fibers through which the ink can pass when the stencil is placed on the cylinder of the reproducing machine. As ink passes through the typed perforations, clear and accurate reproductions of the original are produced.

The A. B. Dick and the Gestetner are excellent stencil duplicators.

The offset process is based on the fact that grease and water do not mix. The outlines on the master copy hold the printing ink, which is greasy, and the remainder of the surface attracts water and repels the ink. The ink is transferred or offset from the outline to a rubber blanket; this is what transfers the copy onto the paper. The plate may be a thin metal sheet or a paper mat, and copy may be photographed onto the plate. Popular offset duplicators are the Addressograph Multigraph, Rotaprint, and A. B. Dick. This equipment is making inroads into many plant reproduction departments in view of the original-like copies reproduced, its multicolor capabilities, and its fast operating speed.

Photocopying duplicators are so nearly automatic that they hardly require the services of skilled operators. A picture of a letter or other document may be reproduced in as little as one minute. Most of the major equipment companies are producing photocopy equipment. The most common photocopy duplicator is the Xerox, although other companies are strong competitors.

Data-processing Machines

The past ten years have seen the widespread use of electronic computers in many offices. Electronic data-processing systems usually consist of a combination of units including input, storage, processing, and output devices. They receive scientific or business data at electronic speeds with self-checking accuracy.

Input devices read data on punched cards, magnetic tape, paper tape, or magnetic discs. The data can be stored in the computer on magnetic cores, magnetic drums, magnetic discs, and magnetic tapes.

The processing unit controls and governs the complete system and performs the actual arithmetic and logical operations.

Output devices record information from the computer on

cards, paper tape, magnetic tape, or as printed information on paper.

The computer cannot reason or think for itself and is unable to perform even the simplest operation without definite instructions. A person must be specially trained to set up the wires controlling the operation of the machine. The person who sets up the machine for analyzing data is called a programmer.

Data-processing equipment is manufactured by International Business Machines, Minneapolis-Honeywell, Univac, Control Data, Burroughs, and NCR. Other office equipment manufacturers also have entered this field.

Calculating Machines

The adding-listing machine is probably the most common type of calculating machine found in the office. On a "listing" machine, the figures are printed on a paper tape so that there is a permanent record which can be checked for errors. There are ten-key machines on which the keyboard consists of one set of keys from zero to nine and full keyboard machines with each column containing keys from one through nine. Adding machines are used primarily for addition and subtraction and are cumbersome for multiplication and division.

Calculating machines record totals in the dials, from which they may be copied. They are used for addition, subtraction, multiplication, and division—all of which are practically automatic. The operator merely sets the figures on the machine and presses the proper key; the answer appears in the proper dials. Emphasis in the offices today is on the desk-size 10-key electronic calculator. Some calculators have the capacity to perform operations in multiplication and division in milliseconds, as well as square roots and statistical operations. Pocket-size calculating machines have become very popular, too.

The more sophisticated calculators have computer-like ability to store instructions, a TV-like screen or illuminated dials to display results, and automatic decimal control.

Burroughs, Monroe, Olympia, Canon, NCR, Hewlett-Packard, and Texas Instruments manufacture many of the calculators now in use.

Not all clerks operate all of these machines. However, it is likely that a clerk will use some of them. Their operation may be learned in school, at training centers organized by the equipment manufacturers, or on the job. Proficient office machine operation is becoming increasingly important as the office becomes more and more mechanized.

Chapter 3

RECORDS MANAGEMENT:
FILE CLERK TO RECORDS MANAGER

Records management is the term used for a system of control in a company that collects, processes, stores, retrieves, disseminates, and disposes of data. The information explosion and the vast amounts of paperwork created in this electronic age have led to the creation of records centers as a vital part of a company's management program. As the volume of records grew from the mountains of information poured forth from the computer and from the expansion of large-scale industry and governmental offices, clerical forces also grew to handle this paperwork, simultaneously adding new dimensions to the filing process.

Records are all documentary materials that are created or received in connection with some activity or transaction. Certain legal documents must be preserved for a stipulated period of time, while others are kept as evidence of decisions, functions, procedures, or policies used in a given situation. The many records that are commonly filed in business are correspondence, legal documents, reports, inventory lists, bank statements, price lists, maps, charts, catalogs, newspaper clippings, personnel records, committee reports, and minutes. Records and information storage can be on paper, cards, punched cards, computer tapes, microfilm, microfiche, or magnetic discs.

The terms *filing* and *records management* frequently are confused. Filing is the process of arranging and storing materials according to some definite plan for immediate access and for permanence; most filing jobs are clerical in nature. Records management is actually the life cycle of a record. This cycle includes the creation, design, processing, and disposition of records in conjunction with the selection of files and equipment and the orientation and training of employees. Records management jobs are classified as managerial.

Most office workers, including supervisors, managers, and executives, do some filing. In small firms, the work is usually performed by the secretaries and stenographers; in large firms, clerks usually do the bulk of the filing. These large firms have centralized records areas.

Since businesses of every size use records, filing jobs can be found almost anywhere in the United States. Some of the specialized job titles for entry-level work are: coding clerk, records clerk, unit clerk, sorting clerk, correspondence file clerk, and file clerk. The Bureau of Labor Statistics describes the levels of file clerks as follows:

Clerk, File I

Performs routine filing of material that has already been classified or which is easily classified in a simple serial classification system (e.g., alphabetical, chronological, or numerical). As requested, locates readily available material in files and forwards material; may fill out withdrawal charge. May perform simple clerical and manual tasks required to maintain and service files.

Clerk, File II

Sorts, codes, and files unclassified material by simple (subject matter) headings or partly classified material by finer subheadings. Prepares simple related index and cross-reference aids. As requested, locates clearly identified material in files and forwards

material. May perform related clerical tasks required
to maintain and service files.

Some of the responsibilities of the specialized clerks are:

Correspondence File Clerk

Maintains a file of general correspondence; sorts
and files; answers inquiries about correspondence;
maintains a follow-up file; labels folders; retrieves
correspondence; and maintains an activity-count record.

Sorting Clerk

Handles notices of change; distributes changes to
unit clerks; alphabetizes information on new accounts; sorts outgoing interoffice communications;
types envelopes; and routes caption changes and
changes of address to the central file records.

Unit Clerk

Maintains an alphabetical unit of customer cards;
answers inquiries about customers; processes reports
and data about accounts; handles signature cards for
the file; checks against file for titles of officers of
customer accounts; and removes cards from unit file
according to a retention schedule.

Coding Clerk

Codes information obtained from reports for
processing by machines.

Records Clerk

Receives company records and examines contents
to determine filing captions; maintains a card file of
records by date for destruction; locates information

in central files upon request; and assists supervisor in organization of records and filing procedures.

Records Manager

Supervises and trains personnel in maintenance of central files; supervises work of employees and evaluates performance; improves personnel relations in the records management department; keeps monthly records of activity; performs miscellaneous duties.

Promotional opportunities are available to the alert, well-trained clerk who knows how to file and control records. The employee who uses initiative and demonstrates leadership qualities may rise from the entry-level job of file clerk to the position of file supervisor, file consultant, or the highly responsible position of a records manager. Most employers follow a promotion-from-within policy.

EMPLOYMENT AND SALARIES

In 1974, approximately 275,000 file clerks were employed; projected estimates for 1985 indicate there will be a demand for 318,000 such employees. Although the increased demand for record-keeping will result in job openings, the growth rate is not expected to be as rapid as in past years because of the increasing use of electronic computers for filing and retrieving information.

File clerks are the foundation of the records system of a business; however, in spite of their vital function, they are among the lowest paid office employees. Of the twelve clerical work levels surveyed by the Bureau of Labor Statistics, beginning file clerks I were at the bottom salary level, earning an average of less than $500 per month. Experienced file clerks III received salaries above accounting clerks I but below accounting clerks II; above keypunch operator I but below keypunch operator II; and above typists II. The average annual salary for the year ending March, 1975, was $5,524 for file clerk I; $6,244 for file clerk II; and $7,683 for file clerk III. The average salary increase for this same period was 9.6 percent, the same as that for the total clerical and clerical supervisory occupations. (See Chart 8.)

CHART 8
Average Salaries For Clerical Occupations*
March, 1974 — March, 1975

Job Title	Annual Salary	% Increase in Average Salary
Clerks, Accounting I	7,141	7.7
Clerks, Accounting II	8,981	
File Clerks I	5,524	
File Clerks II	6,244	9.6
File Clerks III	7,683	
Keypunch Operators I	7,114	9.9
Keypunch Operators II	8,193	
Messengers	6,214	10.1
Stenographers, General	7,801	11.6
Stenographers, Senior	8,784	
Typists I	6,365	9.9
Typists II	7,452	
Keypunch Supervisors I	9,187	
Keypunch Supervisors II	10,595	8.7
Keypunch Supervisors III	11,971	
Keypunch Supervisors IV	14,310	

* Bureau of Labor Statistics, *National Survey Of Professional, Administrative, Technical And Clerical Pay* (Bulletin 1891), March, 1975.

EDUCATIONAL REQUIREMENTS

Most employers prefer to hire high school graduates for beginning file clerk jobs. They prefer applicants who can type, have a knowledge of office practices, have an aptitude for numbers, have the ability to do detailed work accurately, and are able to read quickly and with understanding. In addition, employees should understand the importance to management of accurate files, the necessity to follow organized procedures, and the importance of teamwork. Good clerks have manual dexterity, good eyesight, and good memories. Since file clerks have access to the confidential records of the company, they should possess the personal qualifications expected of other office workers—loyalty to the firm and ability to keep confidences.

HOW FORMER STUDENTS VIEW THEIR TRAINING IN RECORDS MANAGEMENT

In a follow-up study to determine the importance of records management training, 150 college students who were out of school from one to four years were surveyed.* Eighty-five percent of the respondents indicated that they are actively involved with the records of their company; some of their records management responsibilities are:

Job Activities	Percentage of Respondents
Set up a filing system	73%
Use files for filing and retrieval of papers	95%
Creation of records	93%
Transfer records to storage	70%

*Galen Stutsman, "Survey Stresses Need for Filing Instruction," *The Journal of Business Education,* March, 1974, p. 263.

Follow retention schedules	58%
Work in inactive storage areas	43%
Work with vital records	38%
Work with microfilm	20%
Use mechanized equipment	8%

The quotations that follow indicate how important these former students believed the study of records management was during their school years:

"The study of recordkeeping is vital to my work and I believe to every good secretary."

"I feel it is a vital course. . . . When I started working in both the accounting department and the advertising department, the filing system was a mess. There seemed to be no logical reason for the way things were filed . . ."

"Not enough stress can be put on the basic alphabetic and numeric filing systems."

"The job should not really be classified at the bottom of the list as it is in many organizations because the records of a company are its most important and only source of pertinent information, especially after others leave the organization. Studying the subject and knowing the importance of good records is vital, no matter what job one has. No one ever gets completely away from filing or using files in any business."

Chapter 4

WORD PROCESSING—
THE STENOGRAPHER AND THE SECRETARY

Getting words into usable printed form is one of the largest aspects of office work. The two most common job titles in the word processing category are *stenographer* and *secretary*, the subject of this chapter. The characteristic that distinguishes *clerk* from *stenographer* and *secretary* is the use of shorthand. Stenographers frequently are classified as junior (or general) and senior. The promotion ladder is usually from junior stenographer to senior stenographer to secretary.

According to the *National Survey of Professional, Administrative, Technical, and Clerical Pay* (Bulletin 1804, U.S. Department of Labor, Bureau of Labor Statistics), the specific tasks performed by stenographers or secretaries in the three classifications are:

Stenographer, General — Primary duty is to take and transcribe dictation from one or more persons either in shorthand or by Stenotype or similar machine, involving a normal routine vocabulary. May also type from written copy. May maintain files, keep simple records or perform other relatively routine clerical tasks. May operate from a stenographic pool. (Does not include transcription machine work.)

Stenographer, Senior — Primary duty is to take and transcribe dictation from one or more persons either in shorthand or by Stenotype or similar machine, involving a varied technical or specialized vocabulary, such as legal briefs or reports on scientific research. May also type from written copy. May also set up and maintain files or keep records, etc. . . . Performs stenographic duties requiring significantly greater independence and responsibility than stenographer, general. Work requires high degree of stenographic speed and accuracy, a thorough working knowledge of general business and office procedure and of the specific business operations, organization, policies, procedures, files, workflow, etc. Uses this knowledge in performing stenographic duties and responsible clerical tasks.

Secretary — assigned as personal secretary, normally to one individual. Maintains a close and highly responsive relationship to the day-to-day work activities of the supervisor. Works fairly independently, receiving a minimum of detailed supervision and guidance. Performs varied clerical and secretarial duties usually including the following:

- Receives telephone calls, personal callers, and incoming mail; answers routine inquiries; routes technical inquiries to the proper persons;
- Establishes, maintains, and revises the supervisor's files;
- Maintains the supervisor's calendar and makes appointments as instructed;
- Relays messages from supervisor to subordinates;
- Reviews correspondence, memoranda, and reports prepared by others for the supervisor's

signature to assure procedural and typographic accuracy;
- Performs stenographic and typing work.

The definition of secretary adopted by the National Secretaries Association (International) refers more to the personal qualities required for success than to the specific tasks enumerated above. A secretary is:

> "An assistant to an executive, possessing mastery of office skills and ability to assume responsibility without direct supervision, who displays initiative, exercises judgment, and makes decisions within the scope of her authority."

Within this concept, a secretary is a highly qualified person who possesses not only "mastery of office skills" but also personality requisites of the highest order. She discharges the responsibilities for which she has authority, and she is a creative, responsible individual capable of making many decisions.

The stenographer and the secretary both need certain competencies to perform their tasks. They must:

- Understand words and their correct use in business communication;
- Hear phonetic sounds and record them in some type of shorthand;
- Take dictation from an individual;
- Typewrite from dictation, from own notes, and from rough drafts;
- Use correct English mechanics (spelling, punctuation, usage);
- Understand letter, memorandum, and business forms;
- Use specialized business vocabulary required in the work station;

- Record and follow instructions;
- Communicate verbally with superiors and fellow workers;
- Adapt to routine work. (There is routine work in every job, but there is more of it at the lower levels.);
- Analyze incoming mail to use correct address in reply;
- Proofread the material typed;
- Make corrections in typescript;
- Understand the operation of the company, its organization pattern, and the office procedures it follows;
- Understand the established flow of work.

EMPLOYMENT OUTLOOK FOR STENOGRAPHERS AND SECRETARIES

One of the most important considerations in choosing a vocation is the probability that jobs will be available when the training necessary for entering the job in completed. A person has only to look at the openings for stenographers and secretaries in the help-wanted columns of the daily newspaper to see that there is a great shortage of such personnel. For instance, even when New York City was experiencing 10 percent unemployment, on a "light" day there were 30 openings advertised for secretaries versus 6 advertisements for typists and 26 for bookkeepers.

A periodic check of this sort will indicate local needs, but even more reliable is the work of the U.S. Labor Department in studying where jobs will be found in the next ten years. Its 1975 publication, *Occupational Manpower And Training Needs,* unveils employment estimates in 240 occupations. This study estimates that of the more than 10 million clerical jobs estimated to exist in 1972, more than 3 million were in the stenographer-secretary classification; this compared with about a million

CHART 9

Percentage of New Workers Needed
Annually Until 1985

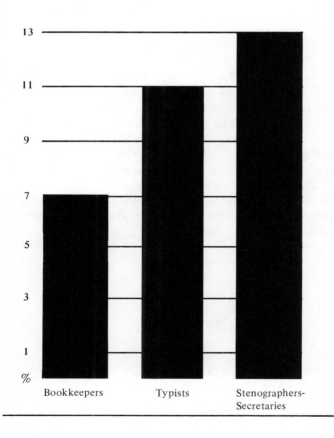

typists and a million and a half bookkeeping workers. But more important than these employment figures are the estimates of job openings for stenographic-secretarial workers *every* year up to 1985—more than 400,000 new workers will be needed! No other group of clerical workers has as large a percentage of increase in openings as secretaries-stenographers—7 percent for bookkeepers and 11 percent for typists.

SALARIES

An annual survey of office salaries in the New York City area by the New York City chapter of the Administrative Management Society (AMS) provides information about salaries of stenographers. Of course, salaries in large cities are usually higher than those in small towns, but they give some idea of how the salaries of stenographers and secretaries compare with other office workers. (Incidentally, the highest salaries for office work are paid in the West, not the East.)

In 1975, parts of reports to AMS from 106 different companies employing more than 78,000 office workers show the following average weekly salaries:

Systems Analyst	$322
Programmer	280
Secretary A	205
Computer Operator A	197
Accounting Clerk A	183
Secretary B	176
Bookkeeping Machine Oper.	170
General Clerk A	163
Correspondence Secretary	158
Stenographer	155

CHART 10

Secretarial Salary Levels

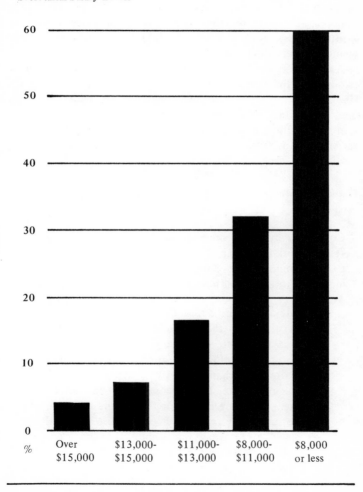

It is significant that, with the exception of systems analyst and programmer which are usually classified as professionals, Secretary A leads the salaries of the office force and Secretary B and Stenographer are in the first eleven groups of office workers in terms of salary. And, according to IBM, secretarial salaries have risen 68 percent since 1965.

A final comment about salaries refers to a 1975 survey of members of the National Secretaries Association (International). The salaries of these seasoned professionals who had been employed as secretaries for at least five years indicate that more than half of them make more than $9,000 a year and that a few make over $15,000.

WHAT SECRETARIES SAY ABOUT THEIR JOBS

Comments by two secretaries attest to their convictions that secretarial work is a rewarding career.

Clare Jennings, past president of the National Secretaries Association (International), puts it this way:

"Only a little more than fifty years ago, the young women who mastered a machine just coming into wide use and who ventured into the then almost entirely male world of business were known as "typewriters." Perhaps that is why many people still have the impression that a secretary's main task is a machinelike turning out of perfect letters from nine to five and why so many others use the title "secretary" to mean anyone employed in any stenographic or clerical position.

"True, typing and shorthand are two of the basic skills of the secretary, but her duties cover a much wider field than the work of such valuable specialists

as the typist, stenographer, file clerk, and receptionist. The secretary, as we use the title today, often fills
all of those positions. In addition, she is an assistant
who knows many of the confidential matters of her
office and of her employer's business dealings. She
uses this knowledge to protect [the employer] from
unnecessary interruptions, delays, and confusions,
and to clear decks in a score of other ways.

"She knows which calls to route to [the employ-
er] immediately, which to delay until she can supply
needed reference material, which she can best deal
with herself. She sits in on conferences when a
trusted witness is needed. Her manner over the
telephone and to visitors sets the mood of the office.
She is a daytime hostess rather than a receptionist.

"One secretary may handle a great volume of
letters; another does very little typing. Under any
circumstances, there is little machinelike about their
work. No machine has the tact to soothe the ruffled
feelings of an important caller who must cool his heels
while an equally important one overstays his time. No
machine has the judgment about what information
may be released in a boss's absence, which requests
must be smoothly sidetracked. No machine can act
as a boss's memory by combined use of intelligence,
filed material, and a carefully kept appointment
book.

"A secretary's career can have enormous personal
rewards. Her working hours and conditions are
pleasant. Her office is certain to be comfortable. In a
big office, she has opportunity to meet many new
friends. Her work puts her in touch with men and
women of achievement in many fields. And no field
of special interest is closed to the young [person]
who chooses secretaryship as a career."

Ann Fallon, secretary to the president of an international oil company and former "Secretary of the Year," says:

> "A secretarial job brings prestige as well as an opportunity to get into an interesting field, such as law, without having to be a lawyer.
>
> "A secretary must enjoy working with people and doing things for them. . . . A well-educated secretary is capable of taking over a lot of work that the boss would otherwise have to do, relieving him of routine items so that he can use his time to better advantage . . .
>
> "The most important qualification is that a secretary be able to get along with people. Especially to be avoided is an officious manner and an inflated idea of one's importance, which puts the boss in a bad light. A secretary must be able to work under pressure. He or she must be able to work without supervision, to take a job and get it done.
>
> "Secretaries must be flexible in different situations, well-rounded, and well-read. It is important to get as much education as possible."

PROMOTIONAL OPPORTUNITIES FOR SECRETARIES

For some, secretarial work can be a satisfying, lifetime occupation; for others, it is a stepping stone to another career. For many years, it was the only way for a woman to get her foot in the executive door.

The 1970s have seen phenomenal changes in the employment picture. One of the most important reasons for increased opportunities for women has been Affirmative Action legislation which compels companies involved in federal government contracts to end discrimination against employment and promotion of women and members of other minority groups. Undoubtedly, many an executive faced with the possibility of court action for violations has looked around for possible candidates for promotion and has promoted a female secretary whose quality of performance is already known.

A sampling of former secretaries who were promoted in 1975 attests to this point. Elinore Stieha of Rapid City, South Dakota, was appointed Assistant to the President of Black Hills Power and Light Company; Phyllis Spencer was made Manager, Personnel Administration, of the Oakland, California, plant of Sherwin-Williams Company, paint manufacturer; Carmen Martinez became Purchasing Assistant for the Raytown, Texas, chemical plant of Exxon Corporation; Mary Holstad was appointed to the Iowa Commerce Commission. Others who began their careers behind the secretary's desk and reached top management are: Marion Stephenson, vice-president of NBC; Josephine Shaeffer, a top executive in a large real estate company in New York; and Virginia Rehme, vice-president of a St. Louis bank.

In all fairness, though, it must be pointed out that new entry-level management jobs for women are opening up. Women are being hired for more and more jobs in all categories of the business world, including management. A woman secretary today will find new competition with other women who earn their advancement via another career path.

LIMITING FACTORS IN SECRETARIAL CAREERS

In the traditional secretarial framework, the secretarial title follows the boss's title not the worker's ability. The secretary is sometimes rated a Secretary B rather than a Secretary A because of the status of her superior, not because of her competence.

Another limiting factor is the difference in concept of the word *secretary*. To attract applicants, a company will advertise for a secretary when the work is purely stenographic or even clerical. Then, too, *secretary* is a status symbol. Who ever heard an employer speak of "my stenographer" or "my clerk"? No, the reference is always to "my secretary." Even within a company, the executives have such a different concept of the term that one boss will assign a wide range of responsibilities while another will make such limited use of the secretary's abilities that the job becomes frustrating.

The final limiting factor is the necessity for the secretary to submerge herself in her employer's problems. As one secretary said candidly, "If I ever quit, it will be because I'm tired of thinking other people's thoughts and want to work on my own." The secretary is working with somebody else's ideas and is the instrument through which these ideas are presented and implemented.

EDUCATIONAL PREPARATION

Stenographic-secretarial preparation is given at all educational levels from the high school up. Most high schools offer a specialization in this field. The usual curriculum includes, along with some non-specialized courses, English (three or four years), possibly including a course in business writing; typewriting (two years); shorthand and transcription (two years); secretarial practice (one year or one semester); bookkeeping (may be omitted); business mathematics (may be omitted). Some schools vary this basic curriculum with inclusion of such courses as personal and business adjustment, data processing, business law, or business organization.

Recent innovations in high school business preparation include block programs of two or three periods replacing the usual 40- or

50-minute class. Under this reorganization, classwork more nearly approximates actual office conditions; additionally, it permits the student to work at a task until it is completed rather than having to break off with the job half finished and possibly never completed. Many schools are offering advanced work through projects involving *simulations* in place of advanced typewriting and shorthand. In simulation projects, the school jobs resemble real office jobs, and the student can see the relationship between the job he or she is performing and the jobs of the other office workers. One of the advantages claimed for simulations is that the student receives training in office behavior, an aspect often overlooked in the traditional classroom.

Since the 1960s, two-year community colleges have grown into a major training ground for secretarial students. Since one of the objectives of these colleges is preparation for semiprofessional jobs, practically all of them offer a secretarial program. One such program, which is offered at Bronx Community College in New York City, is reproduced below.

Curriculum Pattern for Executive Secretary Option

First Semester	**Third Semester**
Course Title	*Course Title*
Fundamental Composition	Art or Music course
History of Western Civ.	Business Communications
Shorthand 1 (Gregg or Pitman)	Shorthand III
Business Mathematics	Typing III
Typing I	Business & Commerce Elective
Fundamental Communications	Free Elective
Second Semester	**Fourth Semester**
Human Physiology	Shorthand IV
Physical Ed. (choose one)	Secretarial Practice
11th Year Mathematics I	Cooperative Work Exp. I
Fundamental Accounting I	Business & Commerce Elective
Shorthand II	Social Science Elective
Typing II	Free Electives
Career Orientation	

In addition to public junior colleges, private junior colleges offer one- and two-year secretarial programs. Private business colleges, many of them accredited as junior colleges, are a primary source for business training. In many private business schools, a student may enroll at any time, not necessarily at the beginning of the term, and may progress at his or her own rate.

In addition to the school programs already described, secretarial courses are offered in almost all adult education programs—at the YMCA, in evening high schools, in churches, in lodges, and wherever self-improvement is the goal. Business organizations are also forced by the shortages of stenographers and secretaries to offer in-service courses. It is not uncommon for clerks to pursue company courses in shorthand and typewriting in the hope of promotion to new jobs in the field; stenographers frequently are sent to company-sponsored courses in English grammar.

SPECIALIZED SECRETARIAL JOBS

Four secretarial positions require specialized abilities: public stenographer, legal secretary, medical secretary, and technical secretary.

Public Stenographer. The secretary interested in working "on her own" may open an office as public stenographer. The office is usually located in a hotel near prospective employers who need special services, usually in a hurry. The public stenographer serves only those who bring work to her; and because she usually does only small jobs for a traveling population of employers, she can charge rather high rates for piecework. A public stenographer is usually also a notary public, one authorized by the state to witness signatures. For this service, she receives a small fee. Much of her work is of a legal nature, and a secretary contemplating a career as a public stenographer should be experienced in legal work.

The major advantages of becoming a public stenographer are freedom from supervision and a wide variety of work assignments. One never knows what type of job will be brought in. If the public stenographer is located in a good spot, she may expect to make a good salary.

The disadvantages of becoming a public stenographer are the instability of employment and the possibility of low income in a poor location, during holiday periods, or in slack seasons. Public stenography demands a high degree of skill and flexibility, too, for each new dictator is new, with unique demands and requirements.

Legal Secretary. Because the vocabulary of law is highly specialized and matters of form and procedure so complicated, many community colleges offer special courses in legal stenography along with special content courses that give legal background. On the other hand, many regular secretaries receive their specialized training in legal work from legal secretaries where they work.

The work of the law office is exacting; an inaccurate record can be extremely expensive. The hours are long, and much of the work is done under pressure. It is no surprise, then, that legal secretaries are among the highest paid in the field.

Medical Secretary. Courses in medical shorthand also are given in community colleges for the medical secretary, who must know not only the shorthand outlines and spelling for medical terms but also their meanings. In addition, she may act as receptionist for the doctor and may even handle billing. Many medical secretaries also perform such medical duties as taking temperatures and blood pressures.

The Technical Secretary. The "tech sec" works for the scientist or the engineer, employers who are at home in the laboratory but not in the office. They are likely, then, to leave much of the organization of the office to the secretary and expect her to handle much of the routine. In addition to usual secretarial duties, she prepares most of the mail from composition to mailing, maintains the technical library, gathers materials for scientific papers and types and edits them, and is more of an assistant than secretary. The engineering secretary checks specifications in contracts against standards and orders the materials that meet the specifications. The work is very demanding, but the pay is high. A good knowledge of and interest in mathematics and science are useful assets for the "tech sec."

PROFESSIONAL ORGANIZATIONS
IN THE SECRETARIAL FIELD

The National Secretaries Association (International) has a membership of more than 35,000 secretaries in its 750 chapters. This organization holds meetings and workshops at the local, state, and national level that are planned to improve the secretarial performance of its members. It sponsors a Future Secretaries Association program, mostly at the high school level, to inform students about the secretarial profession and to interest them in entering the field.

In addition, it is responsible for the Certified Professional Secretaries' (CPS) program, which is an effort to recognize top-level secretaries as separate from so-called "secretaries." Each year, the Institute for Certifying Secretaries administers a two-day examination in six areas of business in centers located in the United States, Canada, Puerto Rico, and Jamaica. The areas covered by the examination are: Environmental Relationships in Business, Business and Public Policy, Economics and Management, Financial Analysis and the Mathematics of Business, Communications and Decision Making, and Office Procedures. Information about the CPS examination may be obtained from the Institute for Certifying Secretaries, a Department of the National Secretaries Association (International), 2440 Pershing Road, Suite G10, Kansas City, Missouri 64108.

The examination is primarily for qualified, experienced secretaries, but students enrolled in two- or four-year colleges may take the examination during their last year. Even if they pass the examination, however, they may not be certified as CPS's until they have acquired two years of secretarial experience.

In the 25 years since its inception, almost 10,000 secretaries have been certified. Because of the difficulty of the examination, secretaries preparing for it devote hours or even years to preparation. The program's contribution to management in improved secretarial performance is incalculable. Some colleges give credit for passing the examination and encourage CPS's to complete their formal education Many corporations give some form of recognition to the secretaries when they pass the examination, such as a one-grade promotion or an automatic salary increase. Remember the secretaries mentioned earlier who had received promotions to management positions in 1975? All of them were CPS holders.

Legal secretaries are eligible for membership in the National Association of Legal Secretaries (International), which also sponsors a professional examination and certification program. Educational secretaries may belong to the National Association of Educational Secretaries, a department of the National Education Association with offices in Washington, D.C. This group works for improvement of salaries, retirement benefits, and tenure coverage for its members. It also sponsors a Professional Standards Program designed to upgrade the profession.

Chapter 5

WORD PROCESSING

Although words have been processed ever since paper was produced, the term *word processing* (WP) has been adopted to describe a new concept to improve the efficiency of business communications. It is, according to IBM, "the transition of a written, verbal, or recorded idea to typewritten form." This is done by adopting the systems approach. One group of employees specializes in performing one function and, with the help of automated equipment, achieves greater productivity. Another group performs the other secretarial tasks required by executives.

The equipment that gave rise to the word processing concept was the Magnetic Tape Selectric Typewriter (MT/ST). This first text-editing typewriter had two distinctive features—it could capture keystrokes, recording them on magnetic tape so that they could be retrieved and played back automatically; and it permitted the typist to correct errors by backspacing to erase the error from the tape and typing the correct character. The mag tape machine was followed by the mag card typewriter. On this equipment, a document can be typed onto a card for easy filing and reinserted into the typewriter for automatic production of multiple copies.

From these beginnings, IBM and other manufacturers have made vast improvements. Today, there are several dozen automatic typewriter manufacturers producing machines that sell for $2,000 to $20,000 and more. Because this equipment is expensive—too expensive to be placed at every secretary's desk—it must be used to capacity. It is necessary, therefore, to place it in special locations called word processing centers where specially trained operators do nothing but produce typewritten output. In these centers, words are processed in much the same way that numbers are processed in data processing centers.

Among the remarkable and vast capabilities of word processing equipment are the abilities to display corrected copy on a screen in front of an operator and to merge materials from several sources to produce one document. For instance, one source produces the address, another produces computerized numerical data, and another produces selected paragraphs from a mag card or a series of mag cards. The result might be a letter to a customer using paragraph 7 and paragraph 234 of sample form letters to delinquent customers and a summary of their overdue bills. It also is possible to send material from one word processing center to a distant company location by computer and thus save time in delivery and expense in preparing a hard-copy printout.

In addition to the availability of new equipment, the cost factor has influenced the rapid growth of automated word processing. The cost of producing a business letter in 1975 was $3.79, according to the Dartnell Corporation; others estimated the cost at closer to $5.00. (These estimates included such items as the dictator's time, the transcriber's time, stationery, type-writer, paper, light, heat, and office rent.) Because such operating costs were accounting for an increasing part of overall costs of producing goods every year, management welcomed the economies achieved through automatic word processing.

ORGANIZATION OF A WORD PROCESSING CENTER

In modern information processing systems, the traditional secretary's job is split into two functions: that of word processor in a word processing center and that of the administrative-support

(AS) secretary (sometimes called administrative secretary) in an administrative-support center. Word processing is such a new concept, however, that organization patterns and job titles are not yet standardized. The flow chart and organization charts that follow are, then, only two possible set-ups. Chart 11 illustrates the reorganization of functions when a word processing center is established.

In this plan, the administrative secretary (administrative-support secretary) gets materials ready for dictation, and the principal dictates (may be the administrative secretary herself if the material is routine). In this word processing unit there are four components: the receiving station, which logs in the received dictation; the word processing manager, who decides the order in which work is to be done and assigns the work to individual operators; the correspondence secretary (sometimes called word processor) who operates the power equipment; and the center coordinator, who proofreads the transcripts. The approved transcripts are then sent back to the administrative secretary, who attaches the necessary enclosures and approves the document for signing. The principal signs, and the administrative secretary distributes the output.

Chart 12 shows one actual organization plan for the word processing center in a large firm.

This center operates both day and night to secure maximum use of its equipment. The word processing manager has full responsibility for both day and night operation; the coordinator-scheduler sees that there is an even flow of work to the word processors. Because there have been serious problems with the quality of work produced in this particular center, two proof-reader-trainers are required to check the work of the 12 to 15 correspondence secretaries and to train them to make fewer errors. Because it takes at least six months for a new employee to reach full production capability, trainees are being prepared for permanent assignments all of the time. Messengers provide a link between the WP center and the AS center.

CHART 11

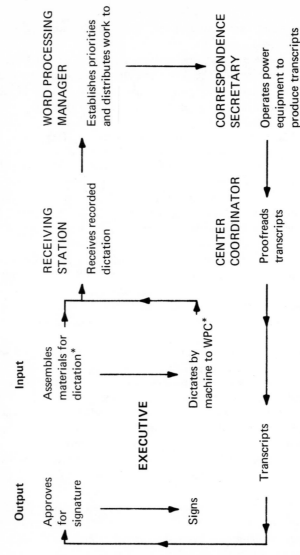

WORD PROCESSING CENTER

ADMINISTRATIVE SECRETARY

WORD PROCESSING MANAGER
— Establishes priorities and distributes work to

CORRESPONDENCE SECRETARY
— Operates power equipment to produce transcripts

RECEIVING STATION
— Receives recorded dictation

CENTER COORDINATOR
— Proofreads transcripts

Input
— Assembles materials for dictation*

Output
— Approves for signature

EXECUTIVE
— Dictates by machine to WPC*
— Signs

Transcripts

*The administrative secretary may also be the originator of dictation.

CHART 12

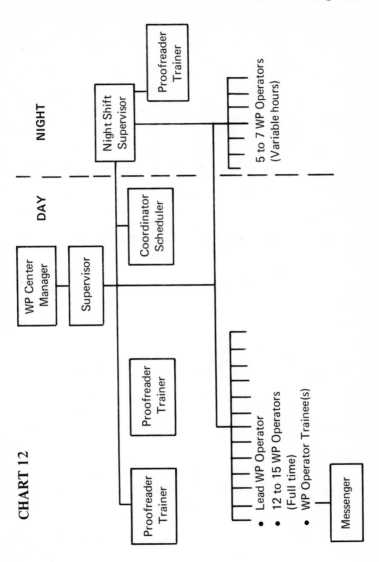

DAY | NIGHT

WP Center Manager
Supervisor

Proofreader Trainer

Proofreader Trainer

Coordinator Scheduler

Night Shift Supervisor

Proofreader Trainer

5 to 7 WP Operators (Variable hours)

- Lead WP Operator
- 12 to 15 WP Operators (Full time)
- WP Operator Trainee(s)

Messenger

Chart 13 shows the organization of the administrative support center in the same organization.

The administrative support manager has responsibility for the operation of the entire center. Under this manager is a supervisor, who sees that the work meets standards. A receptionist and a messenger not only carry out their specialized functions but also serve part-time, along with the full-time administrative aides (administrative-support secretaries or administrative secretaries in other organizations), in performing secretarial responsibilities other than typewriting for several principals. The number of administrative secretaries in a center depends on the needs of the group, but it is possible that six administrative secretaries may serve as many as twenty principals. Administrative secretaries may have general functions for all other-than-typewriting tasks, or they may be assigned special functions in which they excel. For instance, an administrative secretary may perform all records-management functions, all travel-arrangement duties, or all library-research functions for all of the principals in a unit.

QUALIFICATIONS FOR JOBS
IN WORD PROCESSING CENTERS

Jobs in word processing centers will be discussed in the order of their increasing difficulty.

Word Processor or Correspondence Secretary. This operator keyboards in dictation from voice-writing equipment, typing as rapidly as possible and correcting errors by using the typewriter's automatic erasing features. Sometimes the dictator wants only a rough draft so that corrections and changes can be made before a final copy is prepared. Most of the time, though, the keyboarded material is played out into a usable document.

The word processor is responsible, too, for playing out stored mag cards or tapes when the same material is needed again. The

CHART 13

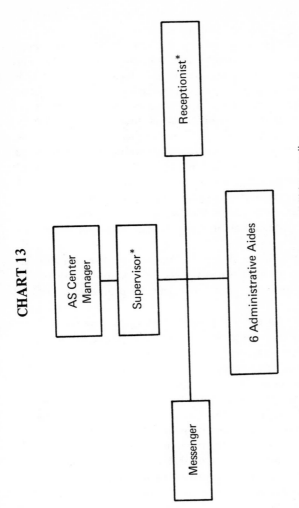

*Supervisor and receptionist have AS responsibilities as well as their respective supervisory and reception duties.

whole document may be reproduced or portions of different stored transcripts may be merged into new output.

Obviously, English skills are very important to the word processor, who must be able to spell and punctuate correctly. The operator must have, to an exceptional degree, the same first qualification required of a traditional secretary—an understanding of words and their correct usage in business communication. Since dictation is from a remote station, there is no opportunity to ask about terms, and the operator cannot make sensible transcripts without a thorough understanding of the business referred to in the dictation. This means that a top-notch word processor must be a highly intelligent person who knows a great deal about the organization's operations. Typewriting speed is not very important; accuracy is. Finally, a word processor must be interested in mechanical equipment and must understand its capabilities.

Proofreader-Trainer. A word processor who is superior in English mechanics and who displays the communications skills necessary for teaching would normally be promoted to proof-reader-trainer.

Scheduler or Logger. The employee who schedules the work of the word processors is a specialized clerk. Some of the items noted on the control sheet prepared in this job are: an assigned number for the job; the nature of the dictation (report, table, instructions, or contract, for instance); nature of the copy (belt, handwritten copy, typing); quality required in output (rough draft or final copy); stationery required; storage (card or tape); length of storage (temporary or permanent); word processor to whom job is assigned; starting time; finish time; number of pages; and time of logging out. To maintain this record, the clerk must not only like detail and be meticulous in accuracy but also be able to make decisions about the output. Another important qualification is the ability to delegate the work of the word processors so that each person does a fair share.

Administrator or Supervisor. Administrative and supervisory jobs require the same competencies needed by anyone responsible for the performance of other workers. They are above the clerical classification; however, they are a possible promotion channel for the word processor. It is important to know, too, that many of the employees chosen to head newly established word processing centers are former traditional secretaries.

REACTIONS OF MANAGEMENT TO WORD PROCESSING

A management consulting company has estimated that WP techniques can usually result in savings of 15 to 30 percent in clerical payroll and overhead for every 100 work stations placed under the program.* One company says that production has doubled with WP—from 250-300 lines a day previously produced by typists at individual work stations to 500-800 lines a day by correspondence secretaries. In another company, ten employees now handle the work previously done by 42. Naturally, management is sold on the concept because of its cost-cutting features.

Management also is happy with word processing systems because they allow secretarial output to be measured. Under the traditional system, the only supervisor of output was the executive for whom the secretary worked; most executives were neither trained in nor especially interested in work measurement. Now, both the administrative support center and the word processing center are manned by someone who does know how to apply quality and quantity measurement standards.

Some executives, who regard their secretaries as status symbols, resist the reorganization of the secretarial function.

---

*Management's Guide To Word Processing, Chicago: The Dartnell Corporation, 1975, p. 15.

They dislike dictating to a machine, and they feel that the whole concept is dehumanizing.

No more than 15 percent of today's offices are organized for word processing; many will never be. Yet progress is being made toward automating the offices of large organizations at lightning speed.

REACTION OF A SUPERVISOR TO WORD PROCESSING

Frances Lewis, Manager of the Word Processing Correspondence Centers of The City University of New York, speaks favorably of the major transition that secretarial services have been undergoing under the name of Word Processing:

> "Word Processing is the better way to handle the communication workload availing itself of the new technology, new procedures, and new organization of personnel. There is no doubt it is the system of the future.
>
> "I believe a slow typist can and will improve speed while using the word processing equipment. However, language skills, such as basic English and its proper use, are a bit more difficult to come by. This is probably the single most important area requiring a student's attention while still attending school and certainly thereafter.
>
> "Our Center secretaries handle jobs for such a variety of departments—legal, academic, administrative, data processing, etc.—that their areas of expertise improve and grow, making them capable of handling diversified documents quickly and intelligently."

REACTIONS OF SECRETARIES TO WORD PROCESSING

The traditional secretary treasures her close relationship with top management. To be successful, she must have a personality that meshes with that of the principal. Her status depends on the job title of the principal, not upon objective evaluation of her work. A secretary who is established in the executive suite is not likely to covet the word processor's job.

More and more secretaries, though, welcome the freedom from routine that automated typing brings. Some of them opt for jobs in word processing centers. They enjoy the opportunities such positions offer for producing larger volumes of higher quality documents, and they like the idea of being "word specialists." Others are attracted to the administrative support center. Although they realize that administrative secretaries have to adjust to the whims of several bosses rather than just one, they see their opportunities for promotion increased in direct proportion to the number of principals they serve. In both cases, they perceive the career paths available within the centers themselves whenever they develop their supervisory and administrative skills.

Most important of all, the office worker of tomorrow must be flexible and ready to accept change. Word processing is bringing the kind of dramatic change that data processing triggered ten years ago. Anyone now in an office job or preparing for one must accept change and adjust to it. In fact, the areas in which changes are occurring are the areas in which the greatest opportunities lie.

SALARIES

Some companies equate salaries of administrative secretaries and correspondence secretaries. They try to make job opportunities parallel between the two centers as workers qualify for more responsible jobs.

In actual practice, however, salaries of word processors are lower than for traditional employees in the secretarial field. According to the New York City Administration Management Society's annual salary survey, the $158 weekly salary of correspondence secretaries was tenth in salary rank among the classifications sampled. The International Word Processing Association confirms that, at the present time, word processors receive comparatively low salaries, but this dynamic association is working for improvement.

IS SHORTHAND OBSOLETE?

A news release from the International Word Processing Association recently stated that "Shorthand skill is becoming an archaic job requirement." Is this statement true?

Want ads for stenographers and secretaries in the daily press and job listings in employment offices refute the statement. The 85 percent of offices without word processing systems refute it too. So do over fourteen hundred members of the National Secretaries Association (International) who have just participated in a survey. They state that of their companies, more than 50 percent require entry-level shorthand speeds of 90 words a minute or more, and 70 percent require typing speeds of 60 words a minute or more. Three-fourths of the secretaries report that they transcribe from symbol shorthand regularly.

But don't administrative secretaries need shorthand, too, even if they do not transcribe their notes into usable business documents? If they can take shorthand, they can save time and be more productive. Secretaries who dictate to word-processing centers can organize their ideas for the dictation into logical sequence by making shorthand notes. Carefully-thought-through letters come back in usable form rather than in rough draft.

The administrative secretary can save time, too, in researching material for reports, in drafting procedures, or in abstracting material if she can make shorthand notes. If she makes notes during interviews with other company personnel, she can provide herself, and often her principal, with exact records. She can take notes in shorthand during meetings and later prepare typewritten proceedings of a conference or a committee meeting. The proceedings or minutes will be available faster if she uses shorthand than if she has to listen to a complete recording. Obviously, shorthand is indispensable for recording telephone conversations, whether the secretary is monitoring a conversation between a principal and an outside caller or is simply taking a message. A final argument for learning shorthand is the advantage it gives the administrative secretary who decides to change jobs. It is often the ace up the sleeve that makes the difference.

As Anderson says, "The business establishment that considers shorthand to be an archaic job requirement has not been studying the productivity of its administrative secretaries. And isn't that productivity what word processing is all about?"*

---

*Ruth I. Anderson, "The Need for Shorthand in the Automated Office," *Business Education World,* January-February, 1976, p. 19.

Chapter 6

THE BOOKKEEPER-ACCOUNTANT

Data is the lifeblood of business that must gather, process, distribute, utilize, and store information. Bookkeeping workers maintain the records of all accounts and business transactions in ledgers and journals and on other accounting forms. The variety of procedures used to process the data range from the simple hand method to electromechanical and electronic methods. Automated equipment and the increasing volume of business gave rise to new job titles for people who process data, such as accountant, auditor, keypunch operator, computer machine operator, systems analyst, and programmer. In each category, there are lines of demarcation reflecting different levels of skills and education as well as specialization tasks. Chapters 6 and 7 give an overview of this occupational field.

Recent statistics show that 1.7 million office workers are engaged in bookkeeping, with another 805,000 employed as accountants. Of this latter group, 20 percent are certified public accountants. (See Chart 14.)

In businesses of yesteryear (and even in some small offices today), a general bookkeeper kept the entire set of books—from journal to balance sheet to profit-and-loss statement. This bookkeeper would analyze and record all financial transactions, balance the accounts, and prepare invoices and payrolls. However, as businesses changed from small, single proprietorships to corporations, the functions usually performed by the one bookkeeper were divided among many workers—each of whom performed a small, routine part of the total operation. For instance, in a large department store today, one clerk may enter charge sales, credit allowances, and payments only for those customers whose names are included in the alphabet from Aa to Av. The clerk who performs this work needs to be a skilled operator of the bookkeeping machine that makes all of the computations. The individual clerk's work is summarized and handed to the head bookkeeper or accountant.

A bookkeeping staff may include a number of such specialized clerks—the entry clerk just described; the ledger or posting clerk, who transfers entries from the various record books into the general ledger containing the complete picture of all transactions; the billing clerk, who mails monthly statements; the payroll clerk; the accounts payable clerk, whose sole concern is with company purchases; and an inventory clerk. In an office employing a number of bookkeeping clerks of varying experience and ability, a head or chief bookkeeper, who may be a fully trained accountant, has charge of the department.

Job opportunities for the bookkeeper exist in all types and sizes of firms, with an exceptionally large number in the wholesale and retail trade. One of every three bookkeepers is employed in a retail or wholesale organization. Other are found in banks, schools, insurance companies, law firms, hospitals, and factories. In banks, bookkeepers are the largest single group of clerks.

Statistics from the 1976-1977 *Occupational Outlook Handbook* show that one in ten clerical workers is a bookkeeper. Chart 14 shows the substantial increase in the number of bookkeeping and accounting employees.

Because of the increasing number of bookkeeping machines and the computerization of recordkeeping, most of the job openings for bookkeepers will result from a high turnover rate because of retirement, death, or other reasons. However, there are shortages of bookkeepers; and the need for bookkeepers during

CHART 14

Number Of Bookkeeping And Accounting Employees*
1972-1985

Job Title	1972	1974	Growth	1985	% of Growth 1972-85
Bookkeepers	1,584,000	1,700,000	116,000	1,900,000	19.5%
Accountants	714,000	805,000	91,000	935,000	31.0%

*Based on data from Department of Labor

the next decade is expected to outpace the impact of laborsaving office machines.

In accounting, opportunities are very good because of the expansion and complexity of business accounting requirements. Morris Diamond, manager of the Professional Placement Center in New York City, said there were very few occupations in which there were more jobs than people seeking them. However, he did cite that the electronic data processing and accounting fields had a great demand for qualified personnel.

The job title, "bookkeeper," causes confusion because it may describe the clerk performing a specific limited bookkeeping function or it may describe a bookkeeper responsible for a complete set of books. The *Dictionary of Occupational Titles* defines bookkeeping jobs as a group of "occupations concerned with computing, classifying, and recording numerical data to keep sets of financial records complete. Occupations concerned primarily with bookkeeping machines, computing machines, and account-recording machines are included." The job descriptions for the two categories of bookkeepers follow:

Bookkeeper (full-charge or general)
    Keeps records of financial transactions of establishment. Verifies and enters details of transactions as

they occur or in chronological order in account and cash journals from items such as sales slips, invoices, check stubs, inventory records, and requisitions. Summarizes details on separate ledgers, using adding machine, and transfers data to general ledger. Balances books and compiles reports to show statistics, such as cash receipts and expenditures, accounts payable and receivable, profit and loss, and other items pertinent to operation of business. Calculates employee wages from plant records or timecards and makes up checks or withdraws cash from bank for payment of wages. May prepare withholding, social security, and other tax reports. May compute, type, and mail monthly statements to customers. May complete books to or through trial balance. May operate calculating and bookkeeping machine.

Bookkeeper (specialized)

Keeps one section of set of financial records, performing duties as described under Bookkeeper I. May be designated according to section of bookkeeping records kept, such as accounts-payable bookkeeper; accounts-receivable bookkeeper; Christmas-Club bookkeeper (banking); interest-accrual bookkeeper (banking); safe-deposit bookkeeper (banking); savings bookkeeper (banking).

A further breakdown of personnel employed in this category are the accounting clerks, a term used by the government synonymously with bookkeepers. The accounting clerk primarily performs the routine accounting clerical operations of posting and verifying as well as preparing journal vouchers. The job descriptions for the two levels of accounting clerks are: *

---

*National Survey of Professional, Administrative, Technical, and Clerical Pay. U.S. Bureau of Labor Statistics Bulletin No. 1891, March, 1975.

Clerk, Accounting

Performs one or more accounting clerical tasks such as posting to registers and ledgers; reconciling bank accounts; verifying the internal consistency, completeness, and mathematical accuracy of accounting documents; assigning prescribed accounting distribution codes; examining and verifying for clerical accuracy various types of reports, lists, calculations, postings, etc.; or preparing simple (or assisting in preparing more complicated) journal vouchers. May work in either a manual or automated accounting system.

The work requires a knowledge of clerical methods and office practices and procedures which relates to the clerical processing and recording of transactions and accounting information. With experience, the worker typically becomes familiar with the bookkeeping and accounting terms and procedures used in the assigned work but is not required to have a knowledge of the formal principles of bookkeeping and accounting.

Clerk, Accounting I

Under close supervision, following detailed instructions and standardized procedures, performs one or more routine accounting clerical operations, such as posting to ledgers, cards, or worksheets where identification of items and locations of postings are clearly indicated; checking accuracy and completeness of standardized and repetitive records or accounting documents; and coding documents using a few prescribed accounting codes.

Clerk, Accounting II

Under general supervision, performs accounting clerical operations which require the application of experience and judgment, for example, clerically processing complicated or nonrepetitive accounting transactions, selecting among a substantial variety of prescribed accounting codes and classifications, or tracing transactions through previous accounting actions to determine source of discrepancies. May be assisted by one or more accounting clerks I.

The question naturally arises at this point as to the difference between a bookkeeper and an accountant. Basically, the difference between an accountant and a bookkeeper centers around the exercise of judgment. The work of a bookkeeper is confined largely to making routine entries in accounting records, without the need of a knowledge of accounting or the exercise of judgment. An accountant, on the other hand, is required to exercise sound judgment in his work. This judgment is based on a sound knowledge of accounting principles and techniques. He is responsible for devising systems and procedures so that the financial affairs of organizations can be recorded and translated into meaningful financial statements, and he must be able to interpret the accumulated data recorded in the organization's books so that proper policy decisions may be made.

In no other clerical field has the increase in the employment of women been so pronounced as in the bookkeeping area. From a completely masculine personnel, the change has been so great that today almost 90 percent of the bookkeepers are women. Increasing numbers of women also are entering the professional field of accounting.

EDUCATIONAL PREPARATION

In choosing workers for bookkeeping jobs, most employers hire people who have completed high school. In coming years, however, many of the jobs opening up in automated offices will require education beyond high school.

Most large high schools have a bookkeeping curriculum to be followed by those interested in vocational preparation for the bookkeeping field. In addition to required courses in English, science, and social studies, the student in a typical program also studies basic or business mathematics, typewriting, business law, business communication, office practice, and two years of bookkeeping.

Community colleges offer accounting specializations which prepare graduates to enter positions as bookkeepers, cost accounting clerks, and junior accountants. Principles of finance, economics, and introductory courses in data processing also are included in the curriculum.

Schools strive constantly to update their bookkeeping and accounting training programs to keep pace with the current trends in the job market. Traditionally, during the first year of training, stress is placed on the mastery of journalizing, posting, and trial balance components. One new program, reported by Hobart Conover of the New York State Education Department, is systems oriented and consists of four modules designed so that students who cannot spend a full year in bookkeeping may complete training modules for jobs in related areas. Module I deals with a typical system in a service business; Module II introduces specialized journals appropriate to a mercantile business; and Module III emphasizes principal bookkeeping subsystems that might be found in a multiple bookkeeper establishment. The student participates in a simulation of the tasks performed by entry-level bookkeepers, such as payroll clerk, accounts receivable clerk, accounts payable clerk, and cashier. In Module IV, the student is responsible for a complete set of books.

Another updated bookkeeping course now includes fundamental data processing instruction, including such courses as steps in data processing, flowcharting techniques, punched cards for preparation of payroll and sale of merchandise, use of magnetic ink character recognition (MICR) in banking operations, and storage of information.

An increasing number of large companies offer on-the-job training on bookkeeping machines to those who have learned bookkeeping operations in schools. Other companies cooperate in work-study programs operated by the high schools, community colleges, and business schools in their locality. The student works for a salary during part of the day and attends related classes during the rest of the day.

Home study or correspondence courses in bookkeeping and accounting have been among the most successful of all courses offered by remote control. Many aspiring accountants, who for one reason or another could not go to college, have obtained very good training by means of home study courses.

THE BOOKKEEPER IN THE AUTOMATED OFFICE

The duties of many bookkeeping workers are likely to change considerably, as more firms make use of bookkeeping machines, electronic computers, and other modern equipment. Nevertheless, a thorough knowledge of basic bookkeeping procedures is still an absolute necessity. Also, since we are living in a numbers-oriented business world, another very important qualification of the bookkeeper is an aptitude for working with figures and for concentrating on detail.

Automation changes not the bookkeeping process itself but the method of performing the process. The work of the bookkeeping cycle is adapted to machine methods. The entire bookkeeping and accounting cycle must be programmed into the machine in a manner that will produce useful financial statements and supplementary reports. It is important that those who operate automatic machines or who work with them in any way be familiar with bookkeeping principles.

HOW TO GET STARTED

Beginning bookkeepers use the same sources of employment as other applicants for positions in the clerical field: the high school or college placement office, the state employment service, newspaper advertisements, suggestions of friends. They are interviewed by a representative of the personnel department and are later sent to the department in which the vacancy exists for an interview.

Clerical ability tests already described may be administered, or specific bookkeeping tests may be given. The National Business Entrance Test in bookkeeping is a very realistic one. The candidates are given a set of books containing entries already partially made; they continue entering the transactions in the proper manner and obtain certain interpretive data from the journals—just as they would continue the work of their predecessors if they took the position.

Many students who have taken part in cooperative programs while in school may find permanent positions in the firms in which they worked as students.

THE WORKING SITUATION

The bookkeeper should have good eyesight, for eyestrain is the principal hazard of the job. Additionally, bookkeepers should develop accurate and legible handwriting and be able to operate the most frequently used bookkeeping machines. Bookkeeping machine operators need manual dexterity and good coordination of eye and hand movements. The hours and conditions of work are similar to those found in other clerical occupations. The work is done in clean surroundings, and good working conditions generally prevail. Along with other office workers, bookkeepers receive fringe benefits (insurance, hospitalization, surgical attention).

Bookkeeping positions provide a worker with the chance to learn the details of business operations. With so much of the work being done on automated equipment, however, it is extremely likely that each bookkeeping employee will be handling only one, or a few, of the many kinds of work necessary to keep a complete set of books. Thus, it may not always be possible to learn the overall picture necessary for complete understanding.

The greatest disadvantage of bookkeeping work, especially in the lower positions, is its lack of variety and its monotony. The extreme specialization in the special bookkeeper's job makes the work routine in nature and definitely unchallenging. Another disadvantage of bookkeeping work is the difficulty of promotion to the accounting level. A bookkeeper's job may be the door to an accounting position only for the person who is interested in attending college at night or on a part-time basis.

SALARIES

A comparative salary survey conducted by the Administrative Management Society in 1975 indicated that accounting clerks do well. The average weekly salary for an accounting clerk B was $151, $19 a week more than a typist-clerk, $34 more than a file clerk, and $15 more than a general clerk B, but $4 less than a stenographer. A bookkeeping machine operator earned $170 per week, only $6 lower than that earned by secretary B, $35 lower than that earned by secretary A, but $30 higher than that made by keypunch operator B and $11 higher than that of the tabulating machine operator. Accounting clerk A earned $183 per week. A comparison of the 1974 and 1975 figures indicated an 11 percent increase in salary for accounting clerk B and an 8.9 percent increase for accounting clerk A, higher than any other category except for stenographer. A look at civil service figures for 1974 showed that bookkeeping workers right out of high school were earning $130 per week, considerably below the figures quoted above. However, the two-year college graduate with some experience earned $163 per week.

ACCOUNTING CAREERS

The normal promotion channel for a bookkeeping employee would be from specialized clerk (entry clerk or bookkeeping machine operator, for instance) to head bookkeeper or supervisor. The climb upward within the company, however, is rather slow. The top jobs in the recordkeeping field usually go to trained accountants who qualify on the professional level.

The highest level of professional skill that may be achieved in accountancy is recognized by a certificate designating the holder as a CPA (Certified Public Accountant). To earn it, candidates must meet various state requirements, including the successful completion of a difficult two-day written examination. The four parts of the uniform CPA examination are Auditing, Commercial Law, Theory of Accounts, and Accounting Practice; but a particular state may also require examination in additional subjects such as economics, taxation, or government accounting. Certified public accountants are the only group of practicing accountants who must demonstrate their competencies by passing the uniform national examination and by meeting other experience qualifications.

Candidates receive credit for the parts of the examination they pass and may retake the sections they fail at a future date. A substantial majority of those who attempt the CPA examination do pass all parts eventually. Although the CPA certificate originally was intended for public accountants as a means of ensuring high-quality services and ethical standards in work involving a public trust, many people who do not intend to practice public accounting take the CPA examination and obtain a license. It can thus be used as a means of securing promotion to bookkeeping (accounting) jobs at the highest levels.

There are 150,000 CPA's nationally, and although most CPA's are men (more than 96 percent), women are gaining in importance in public accounting. Women now have their own national professional society, The American Woman's Society of Certified Public Accountants.

Most states require a four-year college degree as a prerequisite for taking the CPA examination, and the day may not be far off when a college degree will be required in all states. In some states, the educational prerequisite is becoming even more rigid. Florida and Hawaii now mandate five years of education; New York State requires four years of education plus two years of professional experience. A fifth year of education plus one year of experience fulfills the qualifications for candidacy. Many public accounting firms consider only college graduates for positions.

A description of the work of an accountant is given in the *Occupational Outlook Handbook* published by the U.S. Department of Labor:

> Managers must have up-to-date financial information to make important decisions. Accountants prepare and analyze financial reports that furnish this kind of information.
>
> Three major accounting fields are public, management, and government accounting. Public accountants are independent practitioners or employees of accounting firms. Management accountants, often called industrial or private accountants, handle the financial records of their firms. Government accountants examine the records of government agencies and audit private businesses and individuals whose dealings are subject to government regulations.
>
> Accountants often specialize in areas such as auditing, taxes, or budgeting and control. Many

public accountants specialize in auditing (reviewing a client's financial records and reports to judge their reliability). Others advise clients on tax matters and other financial and accounting problems. Management accountants provide the financial information that executives need to make intelligent business decisions. They may specialize in taxes, budgeting, investments, or internal auditing (examining and appraising their firms' financial systems and management control procedures). Many accountants in the federal government work as Internal Revenue agents, investigators, and bank examiners; other government accountants have regular accounting positions.

The American Institute of Certified Public Accountants developed a testing program in an effort to attract qualified young men and women and to provide standards by which their aptitudes can be measured against the demands of a successful accounting career. The tests are made available in three broad service programs known as The College Accounting Testing Program, The Professional Accounting Testing Program, and The High School Accounting Testing Program.

The tests for college students were initiated in 1946. The Orientation and Achievement Tests assist students in deciding whether to choose accounting as a profession and also provide checks at successive levels of advancement throughout the course of accounting study.

The Accounting Orientation Test, High School Level, is designed to provide students, parents, teachers, and counselors with information concerning potentialities for success in the field of accounting or in the general field of business. It yields an "objective appraisal of learning abilities in the verbal and mathematical areas." This is a 50-minute test primarily for high school seniors, but it may be used with juniors also. It measures general aptitude for handling business problems. This test may be of special interest to students who have done well in mathematics or science courses but who may not have considered the opportunities in accounting.

The Level I College Achievement Test is a progress check early in the study of accounting. The Level II College Achievement Test aids seniors in finding employment as accountants by making available standardized measurements of aptitude and proficiency for submission to prospective employers.

At the professional level, tests aid employers in gauging the ability of job applicants and assessing their learning ability. The tests have been used in making decisions regarding retention of temporary workers and in upgrading and promoting permanent staff members.

The computer is having a major effect on the accounting profession. The need for junior accountants will probably be reduced because electronic data processing systems are replacing the manual preparation of records and statements. However, there will be a greater need for accountants to analyze the information made available by these systems.

Electronic devices will help free the CPA from paperwork, thus giving him more time for the interpretive aspects of his assignments. Increased educational requirements for the profession will probably result so that not only a college education but graduate work as well will be a normal part of preparation for accounting leadership.

Accounting is the fastest growing profession in the United States today because of the greater use of accounting information in business management, the complex and changing tax systems, the growth in size and number of business corporations, and the increasing use of accounting services by small business organizations. In government, it is the biggest business of all.

The American Institute of Certified Public Accountants substantiates the foregoing statement and predicts a continued rapid growth of the accounting profession in the foreseeable future for the following reasons:

- The growth of new businesses every year and booming foreign markets assure a sharply competitive economy. In order to compete, businesses will need more cost controls and other studies of management's performance, and more expert help from CPA's in looking ahead.
- More government controls require more sophisticated accounting data and more independent professionals who can take some responsibility for its reliability.
- Businesses will report their financial condition to more investors, creditors, and others.
- Economic, political, and technological developments require experts to develop, analyze, interpret, and communicate economic data.

The Institute recommends accounting careers to those who are good in mathematics and communication skills and who have the right combination of ability, imagination, and willingness to work in a field with varied and almost unlimited opportunities.

SOURCES OF INFORMATION ABOUT PROFESSIONAL ACCOUNTING CAREERS

- The American Institute of Certified Public Accountants (AICPA), 1211 Avenue of the Americas, New York, N.Y. 10036, is a national society serving more than 114,000 members in public practice. The organization provides recruitment materials about the field of accounting; the uniform CPA examination is prepared and graded by the Institute and administered by each state. The AICPA library contains the most comprehensive collection of accounting materials in the United States.

- The U.S. Department of Labor also publishes data about current employment trends in the field.
- The American Woman's Society of Certified Public Accountants was formed in 1933 to promote the interests of qualified women in the field.
- Public accounting is regulated by the state licensing boards, and information about the CPA examinations in each state is available through the state government.

Chapter 7

PROCESSING DATA BY MACHINE

A whole new family of occupations arose as the rapid growth of data processing equipment spread into the areas of government, business, hospitals, professional offices, industries, and education. A new age of data processing ushered in the development of electronic equipment to handle many complex problem-solving jobs, with a reduced expenditure of human energy. These tasks include billing customers, completing payrolls, scheduling the operations of a business, making airline and hotel reservations, taking and maintaining inventory, recording bank deposits and withdrawals, and monitoring factory production processes. However, these machines are just equipment having "artificial intelligence." What is needed are competent, thinking workers at all skill levels to design systems, write instructions, translate data into machine-readable language, operate the computers and auxiliary equipment, retrieve the results, and maintain the systems. The information generated is only as meaningful as the humans that handle the input (the instructions for the computer) and output (results).

WHERE ELECTRONIC DATA PROCESSING
JOBS ARE FOUND

A striking trend of recent years is the use of the small business computer in many areas of everyday life. In the supermarket, the scanner helps the clerk check and bag a product simultaneously; in the hospital, the computer researches and diagnoses a case; in education, computer-assisted instruction individualizes learning; in the government, the Internal Revenue Department evaluates tax returns; and in some courts that are experimenting with computer systems, the computer retrieves data on the criminal status of the defendant, thus assisting the judge in setting bail bonds.

Business is the largest employer of data processing personnel, with the federal government a close second. Typical users are banks; insurance companies; manufacturers such as International Business Machines, Honeywell, National Cash Register, Burroughs, Redactron, and Sperry Rand/Univac; retail merchandising firms; and data processing service organizations.

SPECIALIZED DATA PROCESSING JOBS

A glance at the duties of various electronic data processing workers will give you an idea of the specialties available in the field. Job descriptions given in this section are those used by the Bureau of Labor Statistics and are prefaced by characteristics of the work situation. Generally, workers in data processing must be accurate and precise. Other characteristics essential to a successful career in this rapidly changing field are a willingness to learn continuously, to face challenges, and to be flexible and ready to make changes.

Keypunch Operator. The keypunch operator is a data processing clerk who operates an office machine directly related to the computer that records or verifies alphabetic and/or numeric data on tabulating cards or on tape. Keypunchers and auxiliary equipment operators work under close supervision as part of a team. The work is repetitive; and unless you prefer routine and like working with machines, it can become boring. Frequently, keypunch operators and data typists are tested to determine the degree of accuracy and rapidity with which they work. They may also be required to work nights, especially if they are new employees, since many employers keep the machines in operation 24 hours a day. All operators of equipment should have manual dexterity and mechanical aptitude. They must be able to concentrate well and enjoy working with details. The position is classified into the following levels:

Keypunch Operator I

Work is routine and repetitive. Under close supervision or following specific procedures or instructions, works from various standardized source documents which have been coded and follows specified procedures which have been prescribed in detail and require little or no selecting, coding, or interpreting of data to be recorded. Refers to supervisor problems arising from erroneous items, codes, or missing information.

Keypunch Operator II

Work requires the application of experience and judgment in selecting procedures to be followed and in searching for, interpreting, selecting, or coding items to be keypunched from a variety of source documents. On occasion may also perform some routine keypunch work. May train inexperienced keypunch operators.

Keypunch Supervisor

Supervises three or more keypunch operators who keypunch or verify cards or tape for computer or tabulating machine processing. May also, as an incidental responsibility, supervise the operation of other types of punching machines such as reproducers or

COURIER-JOURNAL & LOUISVILLE TIMES

Competent employees at all skill levels are needed to design data processing systems, write instructions, translate data into machine-readable language, operate computers, retrieve results, and maintain systems.

gang punches. Keypunch supervisory positions are classified in five levels on the basis of combinations of three elements—level and kind of supervisory responsibility, difficulty of keypunch work supervised, and number of employees supervised.

Console Operators must be capable of exercising independent judgment. This personal quality gives them the promotional opportunity to move up to a supervisory position or a job that combines supervision and console operation.

Console operators examine the programmer's instructions for processing the input, make sure the computer has been loaded with the correct cards or magnetic tapes, and then start the computer.

Computer Operator I

Work assignments consist of on-the-job training (sometimes augmented by classroom training). Operator is provided detailed written or oral guidance before and during assignments and is under close personal supervision.

Computer Operator II

Work assignments typically are established production runs (i.e., programs which present few operating problems) executed by serial processing (i.e., one program is processed at a time). In response to computer output instructions or error conditions, applies standard operating or corrective procedure. Refers problems which do not respond to preplanned procedure.

Computer Operator III

Work assignments are characterized by the frequent introduction of new programs, applications, and procedures (i.e., situations which require the operator to adapt to a variety of problems) executed by serial processing. In response to computer output instructions or error conditions, applies standard operating or corrective procedure. Refers problems which do not respond to preplanned procedure.

Data Typists use special machines that convert the information they type into holes in cards or magnetic impulses on tapes or disks. They also may type input material directly into a computer.

Tape Librarians classify and catalog this material and maintain files of program development records and computer operating instructions.

Systems Analysts work with all aspects of computer processing. They plan and organize the information flow from the source to the computer. The more sophisticated positions of programmer and systems analyst are management level jobs which are filled by individuals who enjoy solving problems, have decision-making ability, and can think logically and are able to work with abstract mathematical concepts. Programmers tell the computer what to do. They write the procedures for the computer to follow.

Other jobs. The introduction of electronic data processing systems into banks and the specialized nature of their operations led to the creation of several new clerical occupations that are unique to the banking industry:

Electronic Reader-Sorter Operator — Runs electronic check sorting equipment.

Check Inscriber Or Encoder — Operates machines that print information in magnetic ink on checks and other documents to prepare them for machine reading.

Control Clerk — Keeps close check of large volume of documents entering and leaving the computer division.

Other bank data processing jobs are card-tape converter, coding clerk, printer operator, verifier operator, and teletype operator.

EDUCATIONAL PREPARATION

Most employers prefer that their electronic data processing personnel have some type of specialized training. A high school diploma is a minimum requirement for entry-level jobs, but a college degree and experience are essential for the higher-level positions. Training also is available from manufacturers, private computer schools, and in-house training programs of computer users.

Specialized data processing courses are offered in the high schools, in occupational centers such as BOCES, in junior and community colleges, and in a number of universities and colleges. Data processing vocabulary and a functional knowledge of various data processing concepts, such as flow charting, are included as units of study in related courses. The following is a typical high school curriculum in data processing:

AUTOMATIC BUSINESS DATA PROCESSING

REQUIRED COURSES:

English	4 units	Science	2 units
Social Studies	4 units	Major Sequence	
Mathematics	2 units	in one field	3 units
(Business Mathematics		Physical Education	1 unit
accepted)		Health	½ unit

	9th Year	*10th Year*	*11th Year*	*12th Year*
Basic or Core Courses	Ninth Year Math or	Business Mathematics	Bookkeeping 1 Automatic Data Processing 1	Automatic Data Processing 2
Options (Minimum of one required)	General Business*	Typewriting	Office Practice 1**	Office Practice 2 or Bookkeeping 2 or Business Law or Related Occupational Elective

* Business Communications/Business Foundations may be substituted in Grade 10-11

**Typewriting is a prerequisite

Occupational Objectives:

Tabulating Machine Operator	Digital Computer Operator
Sorting Machine Operator	High-Speed Printer Operator
Coding Clerk (Clerical)	Computer Peripheral Equipment Operator

Overton's study of North Carolina businesses and industries having computer installations and of technical institutes and community colleges with data processing programs revealed that:

- High school is a desirable educational level for computer operators, keypunch operators, data processors, data processing coordinators, and keypunch supervisors.

- Graduates of technical institutes and community colleges may enter the following data processing jobs: computer programmer, data processor, cooperative computer programmer trainee, and data processing coordinator.

- Further education beyond the high school level is desirable for a computer programmer manager, systems analyst, systems manager, and data processing manager.

- Many job opportunities are available for the computer operator, programmer, and keypunch operator.

- Oral and written communication skills are important.

- Recommended courses are: general mathematics, introduction to business and bookkeeping/accounting, introductory courses in automated and electronic data processing.*

EMPLOYMENT PROJECTIONS

From 1960 to 1970, there was a growth of several hundred percent in computer manpower. In 1970, approximately 39 percent were employed as keypunch operators, 19.6 percent as computer and peripheral equipment operators, 23 percent as programmers, and 13.4 percent as systems analysts. The outlook for employment is good through 1985, primarily because:

- Computers are used as management tools.

- The number and types of peripheral equipment manufacturers are growing. (Peripheral equipment, such as high-speed printers, card readers, and card punches, are not in direct

---

*R. Jean Overton, "Business Data Processing Curriculum in the Community Colleges and Technical Institutes and Data Processing Job Classifications in Selected Businesses and Industries in North Carolina," Ed. D. Dissertation, University of North Carolina, 1973.

communication with the central processing unit of a computer.)

- The organizational demand for computers or computer services is becoming larger.
- There will be continued development of new applications.

Although the total number of persons employed in the data processing field is expected to grow to almost one million workers by 1980, the rate of growth will be much slower because of a nationwide economic slowdown, the development of new, less complicated equipment, and greater use of time sharing. The demand for keypunch operators is expected to decline through the mid-1980s because of advances in other data-entry techniques and equipment.

In contrast, advances and expanding utilization of computer hardware and software technology will result in a greater demand for computer and auxiliary equipment operators. Higher levels of applications of computer technology will necessitate the demand for such high-level personnel as systems programmers and systems analysts. From 1970 to 1980, the percentage change anticipated for keypunch operators is -21.7 percent; for computer and peripheral equipment operators, an increase of 83.3 percent; for programmers, 41.6 percent; and for systems analysts, 60.7 percent. (See Chart 15.)

SALARIES

A survey of 125,000 electronic data processing workers by the Bureau of Labor Statistics between July, 1972, and June, 1973, revealed that systems analysts and designers of computer systems earn more than twice as much as individuals who keypunch data for processing by the systems.

CHART 15
Employment Projections
1970-1980*

Occupation	1970 Employment	Projected 1980 Requirements	Percent Change
Keypunch Operator	300,000	235,000	-21.7
Computer and Peripheral Equipment Operator	150,000	275,000	83.3
Programmer	176,500	250,000	41.6
Systems Analyst	102,700	165,000	60.7

*Based on data from Bureau of Labor Statistics

Average weekly earnings, as indicated in an area wage survey of the U.S. from 1972-1973, for a keypunch operator Class A are $132; for a computer operator class A, $185.50; for a programmer class A, $247.50. Figures for March, 1975, indicated a salary for keypunch operator A of $157.50, an increase of 20 percent for the period. Salaries in the metropolitan areas were slightly higher. Most interesting and significant is a comparison of weekly earnings by industry, which reveals that public utilities pay the highest salaries and finance pays the lowest. The differential, or salary difference, for the keypunch operator was $39; for the computer programmer, $38; and for the computer operator, $32. Also significant was the lower salary earned by women for comparable work. The keypunch operator enjoyed the highest rate of increase in annual earnings during the period from 1961-1975, a rise of 5.3 percent compared to the 5.2 percent increase by stenographers; file clerks, 5.1 percent; and typists, 4.8 percent.

WOMEN IN DATA PROCESSING CAREERS

A 77 percent response to a questionnaire on the role of women in data processing that was mailed to 425 women in the

United States who hold professional jobs in the computing field or who use the computers as a research tool showed that women view their roles with enthusiasm. "The computing field attracts, challenges, and rewards the most able women."*

Two-thirds of the women believed they enjoy equal status with men in pay and promotions. Seventy percent believed they could advance to a senior level, but only 56 percent believed opportunities exist for them in management level positions.

The comments made in the survey regarding the position of women in electronic data processing careers included both positive and negative reactions. Some comments were:

> "Women who attain management positions are aggressive, super-competent and competitive, and scorned by males as 'unfeminine' and 'know-it-all' types."

> "Now that I am in higher management, I do not, on my level, see anyone acting threatened—only happy to have someone with whom to share the work and responsibility."

> "If asked about equal pay, the company responds that women are paid in the same range as men. I'm paid at the bottom of the range. Enough said."

> "I think it's a great field—the work is exciting, the salary opportunities are very good. I have never found women being paid less for the same work as happens so often in other fields."

> "I love my work and especially enjoy my half-time arrangement. It's the best of both worlds for a woman with children."

---

*Winifred Asprey and Anne Wheeler Laffan, "Women Speak Out on DP Careers," *Datamation,* August, 1975, pp. 41-43.

". . . lack of promotion is due not usually to overt, conscious discrimination on the part of men but to the rather interesting fact that the thought of promoting a woman simply seems never to occur to them, regardless of how competent she is."

To continue to elevate the status of women in electronic data processing, Asprey and Laffan suggest that more well trained and well educated women enter the field. Secondly, those who are in the field should make themselves heard so that young women students have role models to emulate.

Despite the multitude of unrealized goals and shortcomings within this occupational category, Betty F. Maskewitz, director of the Radiation Shielding Information Center at Oak Ridge, reflects the attitudes of many of the respondents: "Computing is a wonderful field for women—an exciting field for anyone regardless of sex or any other . . . qualifier."

Chapter 8

WHICH TYPE OF ORGANIZATION?

After the selection of the kind of clerical position desired, the candidate continues the job search by taking a personal inventory. Several very important questions on that list should be: In what kind of an office do I want to work—a one-clerk office or a large firm? Do I prefer a job in a business, with a professional person, or in some type of government service? Do I want to work in a city, in a rural district, or in a small town? Do I prefer a centralized office organization such as those found in firms with word processing centers or a decentralized office? Do I prefer a downtown or a suburban location? Would a specific department of a firm be more compatible with my interests and skills? Do I prefer being a big wheel in a small firm or a cog of a wheel in a big firm? Would I be happier performing a multitude of tasks required in a small office or one specific job in a large firm?

THE ONE-CLERK OFFICE

Many clerical workers prefer to work in a one-clerk office. Here they get broad, specific experience in all daily office routines and have such a wide variation of duties that the work seldom becomes monotonous. The one employee handles both incoming and outgoing mail, files, handles cash, makes long distance calls, purchases supplies, makes reports, and acts as receptionist. The small office may be a branch of a national firm

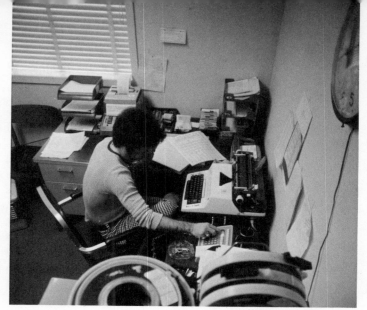

One-clerk offices offer broad experience with a wide variety of duties.

under the supervision of a branch manager, an insurance agency, a real estate office, an employment agency, or a church or school office.

A specialized type of clerical position is found in the office of the professional person—the attorney, the architect, the engineer, or the accountant. In such a position, the clerk may be the only member of the office force or may work with just a few other clerical employees. Special skill in legal work for the lawyer, in writing specifications for the architect, or in checking figures for the engineer or the accountants is required. Such offices usually require a great deal of dictation and typing—with a high degree of accuracy—and tactful handling of clients. The clerk usually keeps a simple set of books, handles the time and expense records of other clerks, and compiles and sends bills. Proficiency in handling figures is required for these positions.

Even more specialized is the clerical work in a doctor's or a dentist's office. A good portion of the clerk's time is spent serving as a receptionist and in keeping patients' records. The ability to master simple nursing techniques might also be expected.

The chief advantage of working in a small office is the absence of work pressure. The office hours usually are standardized, but the clerk can exercise flexibility in planning the work schedule.

The personnel policies are not as clearly specified as in the large office, where it is essential that all employees receive the same treatment. In many cases, this absence of definite policies works to the advantage of the employees, who may leave early, take an occasional day off, or receive an unexpectedly long vacation. Since there usually are no arrangements for sick leaves or emergency absences, concessions for emergencies are often granted. However, in the absence of specified regulations, such advantages are at the discretion of the employer, who may not grant any of them.

The principal disadvantage of working in the one-person office is that there is no room for advancement. The clerk probably receives a salary limited by the amount the small office can afford to pay, and, even though the employee's effectiveness may increase, positions do not exist for promotion. Such salary increases as are given are at the whim of the employer.

THE LARGE OFFICE

The clerk in the large office works with lots of other people; the type of person who enjoys being with a group will be happiest in this environment.

In a large office, the clerk need not have such a wide knowledge of all office routines as the one in the small office needs. For instance, in large offices, the switchboard operator handles some of the telephone duties; the mailroom performs the postal and shipping chores; the purchasing department buys the supplies.

Certain duties, such as filing, typing, stenographic work, duplicating, mailing, machine transcription, calculating work, and messenger service, often are performed by a centralized service department in a large office. Instead of having each department in the office handle these activities individually, one central department is set up for each such activity. Centralized service departments are economical because they eliminate duplication of equipment and files and the need to train operators for limited service in each separate department.

The clerks in the stenographic pool do nothing except take dictation and transcribe it; the clerks in the mailroom do nothing except sort and distribute incoming mail and prepare outgoing mail for sending. Thus, clerks can be trained for specialized work so that they perform with great proficiency and speed. The work is supervised by a trained employee so that the clerk secures superior instruction. The disadvantage of working in a centralized service department is the degree of monotony involved in the work. Another disadvantage is that the employee learns to perform one limited function but nothing else, so that the education received is limited.

Automated equipment of all types is in use in most large offices. Many of the clerical jobs in such places will be rather routine. Special training is usually given by the company to the clerks who will operate this equipment.

Large offices have clearly defined personnel policies which are explained to the worker. During the first day on the job, a manual is distributed which sets forth the hours of work, overtime pay regulations, vacation eligibility, number of days allowed for sick and emergency leaves, holidays, salary range and policies for increases, and plans for merit rating. In addition, large companies offer "fringe" benefits beyond salary which are tax exempt. These may include group life insurance, hospitalization insurance, credit union, stock purchase privileges, pension plan, and bonuses.

Salaries in large companies are often higher than they are in small ones. Increases usually are based on the ability of the worker to produce, and it is possible for a worker with ability to move up into a new job and classification on the basis of merit ratings.

DOWNTOWN, SUBURBAN, AND OUTLYING OFFICES

A job in a small town will probably pay less than one in the city. However, living expenses will also be lower; and some people are happier in small towns than in cities.

The large offices of stores and banks, government agencies, utilities, and similar corporations usually are found in the downtown district. The executive offices of the large corporation also usually occupy a downtown location. In these offices the pace is brisk, the atmosphere sophisticated. The offices usually are supervised by an office manager, and the centralized service units are operated by trained supervisors.

The metropolitan atmosphere makes shopping and entertainment facilities so readily accessible that the workers spend more money than in more isolated surroundings. Also, the employee in the heart of the city spends more for clothing than the worker in the suburban area.

Most of the employees use public transportation to the downtown office because of traffic congestion and high parking costs. The clerk who lives away from home will find living expenses so high that a salary that looked more than adequate will require careful stretching.

Large companies now have been building their factories in suburban areas located along public transportation routes. More casual dress is appropriate in the offices of these companies. Parking facilities are provided, and car pools are operated by employees to reach work. Since food is a problem in these locations, the employing company may provide a lunch that is served free or at cost.

GOVERNMENT JOBS

At one time, the federal government was one of the highest paying employers of beginning office workers. This is not necessarily true today in every category. A glance at the figures in Chart 16 shows the range of salaries for comparable job titles in private industry and in the federal government.

CHART 16
Average Monthly Salaries Of Clerical Workers
In Private Industry And The Federal Government*

Job Title	Private Industry	Federal Government
Accounting Clerk (Beginning)	$551	$499-563
Accounting Clerk (Experienced)	697	633-708
Stenographer (General)	586	499-708
Senior Stenographer (Experienced)	663	688
Secretary	638-690	840
File Clerk (Beginning)	464	499
File Clerk (Experienced)	624	659

*Figures based on data from *Occupational Outlook Handbook,* 1976-77, U.S. Department of Labor.

In order to keep appointments to government positions outside politics, these jobs are secured by taking civil service examinations. Each applicant for a clerical job must pass the written test on verbal and clerical abilities and a performance test of skills. Promotion to the next job level is dependent, too, on passing a promotion examination.

Fringe benefits consisting of paid vacations, sick leave, paid holidays, periodic pay increases, liberal retirement, low-cost life insurance, group health insurance, and incentive awards are evaluated by the job candidate more heavily than in previous years. Clerks interested in foreign travel may secure an overseas civil service appointment for two years. Additional pay is given for out-of-the-country service.

DEPARTMENT ASSIGNMENTS

A new clerk may be assigned to a central service unit or to a special department, such as the sales department, purchasing department, the personnel department, advertising department, or the statistical department. An assignment might also be to some department within the financial division, such as the general bookkeeping department, cost accounting department, tax department, internal auditing department, or the credit department.

One person may be happiest in the duplicating department while another may have little aptitude for machines and detest the work. One person may like the hectic life at the hub of the office activity, the sales office. A clerk with aptitude for figures and an analytic mind may find the work of the statistical department fascinating and have a potential for advancement to the point of designing the tabulating projects.

A clerk who does not like figures would not be happy in one of the financial offices. A clerk who enjoys typing tables is much sought after in the statistical department or in an accounting department.

A clerk who likes people better than figures would fit into the personnel office, where hiring, promotion, and firing take place. A clerk with a creative flair would be stimulated by the work of the advertising department.

In other words, employees should choose to work in a department where the employment will be attractive to them because of their temperament and aptitudes. A square peg in a square hole! There is a place for everyone, but everyone will not enjoy or succeed in the same job.

PART-TIME EMPLOYMENT FOR CLERKS

Employers seek the part-time services of experienced clerks during periods of clerical shortages and peak seasons. Budget-conscious employers keep their operating expenses reduced for the fiscal year by employing temporary help when needed.

Statistics indicate that during 1972, an average of 10.5 million people voluntarily worked less than 35 hours a week. Of the female temporary office workers, 93 percent were high school graduates, 42.7 percent attended college, and 17.6 percent were products of business or technical schools. Seventy percent were married, and 60 percent had children.

Part-time employment can be found in virtually every occupation. There are openings for cashiers, receptionists, stenographers, secretaries, typists, and bookkeepers. Clerical workers constitute the largest number of people holding part-time jobs.

Persons seeking such work register for employment on special rush assignments and are on call when needed. In some cases, the work can even be taken to the home of the part-time worker. One employment agency in New York handles only special jobs and recruits all its workers from the homemaker category.

Many employment agencies supply only temporary office help, persons who do not want steady employment but who still enjoy keeping their hand in office work occasionally. The work provides not only supplementary income but also contact with the stimulating business world. Once you are a trained clerk, you will always be in demand.

Advantages of part-time work are:

- The employee can select time of employment.

- An individual can earn extra money when needed, such as at Christmastime or for a vacation.

- A lonely person can work to be in touch with other people.

- A person has an opportunity to try a variety of jobs.

- A beginning worker gains confidence from this experience.

- An individual has an opportunity to explore different fields.

- The employee has an opportunity to shop around for the "right" job.

The limiting factors in working with a temporary agency are:

- The hourly wage is lower than a steady job would pay.
- Fringe benefits are not given.
- The employee is not eligible for periodic merit increases.
- The individual must constantly adjust to new situations and changing environments.

The average salary range for part-time workers with general office skills is $2.30 to $4.50 an hour; specialized work pays more. If the employee works for a temporary personnel service, the agency pays the salary.

APPENDIX A

RECOMMENDED READING

Accounting, A Career for Women, Too. The American Woman's
Society of Certified Public Accountants, Marysville, Ohio.

Anderson, Ruth I. "The Need for Shorthand in the Automated
Office." *Business Education World,* January-February, 1976,
p. 19.

American Manpower Today. U.S. Department of Labor, Washington, D.C.: 1974.

Asprey, Winifred, and Anne Wheeler Laffan. "Women Speak Out
on DP Careers." *Datamation,* August, 1975, pp. 41-43.

Bellotto, Sam, Jr. "Male Temps: Clerks to Controllers." *Administrative Management,* March, 1971, pp. 54-55, 79-80.

Blackmore, Donald J. "A Salary Profile of Electronic Data
Processing Occupation." *Monthly Labor Review,* March,
1975, pp. 51-56.

"The Computer Manpower Evolution." *Occupational Outlook
Quarterly,* Summer, 1975, pp.28-29.

Crenshaw, Doris C. "Word Processing Can Be A Secretary's Best
Friend." *The Secretary,* November, 1974, pp. 20-24.

Directory of Accredited Institutions. The Accrediting Commission for Business Schools of the United Business Schools
Association, Washington, D.C.: 1971.

Employment and Earnings. Bureau of Labor Statistics, Washington, D.C.: May, 1976.

Equal Pay. Employment Standards Administration, Washington,
D.C.: 1974.

Facing Facts About Vocational Education In Your Career. The Prudential Insurance Company of America, Newark, N.J.: 1975.

"Five Ways to Organize Administrative Support." *Administrative Management,* May, 1974, pp. 22, 83.

Getting The Right Job. SCM Glidden-Durkee, Cleveland, 1973.

A Guide To Your Future In Computer Programming. ITT Educational Services, Inc., 1970.

Hechinger, Fred M. "Education's New Majority." *Saturday Review,* September 20, 1975, pp. 14-18.

Jobs For Which A College Education Is Usually Required. Bureau of Labor Statistics, Washington, D.C.: 1973.

Meisner, Dwayne. "The New Economics of Temporary Personnel." *Administrative Management,* May, 1974, pp. 20-21.

Merchandising Your Job Talents. Manpower Administration, Washington, D.C.: 1974.

Mills, Tom. "Support System for Active Management." *Word Processing,* May/June, 1975, pp. 6-7.

National Survey of Professional, Administrative, Technical, and Clerical Pay. Bureau of Labor Statistics, Washington, D.C.: 1975.

A New Approach To Manpower. Manpower Administration, Washington, D.C.: 1974.

Occupational Manpower and Training Needs. Bureau of Labor Statistics Bulletin No. 1824, Washington, D.C.: 1974.

Occupational Outlook Handbook. U.S. Department of Labor, Washington, D.C.: 1976.

"Occupational Outlook For The Mid-1980's." *Occupational Outlook Quarterly,* Winter, 1975.

Prigge, Lila L. "Specialized Programs in Office Occupations." *Journal of Business Education,* April, 1976, pp. 211-213.

Renee, M. Anne. "What Business Wants From Beginners." *Administrative Management Society Report,* May, 1974, pp. 55-57.

Schmidt, Gary D. "The Small Business Aspect of Bookkeeping/ Accounting." *Business Education Forum,* May, 1976, pp. 22-24.

Short, Larry E. "Nondiscrimination Policies: Are They Effective?" *Personnel Journal,* September, 1973, pp. 786-792.

Stutsman, Galen. "Survey Stresses Need for Filing Instruction." *The Journal of Business Education,* March, 1974, p. 263.

A Working Woman's Guide To Her Job Rights. U.S. Department of Labor, Women's Bureau, Washington, D.C.: 1975.

We Are Involved. The CPA—His Career, His Contribution To Society. American Institute of Certified Public Accountants, New York: 1970.

What Does A CPA Do? American Institute of Certified Public Accountants, New York: 1970.

What's It Like To Be An Accountant? American Institute of Certified Public Accountants, New York: 1970.

"Word Processing, Options Gain Interest Preparing Good Careers." *Lovejoy's Guidance Digest,* February, 1976, p. 4.

MAGAZINES

The National Educational Secretary. Official magazine of the National Association of Educational Secretaries, National Education Association, 1201 Sixteenth Street N.W., Washington, D.C. 20036.

The Secretary. Official magazine of the National Secretaries Association (International), 2440 Pershing Road, Suite G-10, Kansas City, Missouri 64108.

Today's Secretary. Intended primarily for the student training for a secretarial career. Gregg Division of McGraw-Hill Book Company, Inc., 1221 Avenue of the Americas, New York, N.Y. 10020.

BOOKS WITH SUGGESTIONS FOR INTERVIEWS
AND APPLICATION LETTERS

Meehan, James R., Mary Ellen Oliverio, and William Pasewark. *Secretarial Office Practice,* 8th ed. Cincinnati: South-Western Publishing Company, 1972.

Gregg, John Robert, et al. *Applied Secretarial Practice,* 7th ed. New York: McGraw-Hill Book Company, 1974.

Hanna, Marshall, Estelle L. Popham, and Rita Tilton. *Secretarial Procedures And Administration,* 6th ed. Cincinnati: South-Western Publishing Company, 1973.

Morrison, Phyllis. *A Career In The Modern Office,* Book 4, *Getting the Right Job.* New York: McGraw-Hill Book Company, 1970.

Murphy, Herta A., and Charles E. Peck. *Effective Business Communication.* New York: McGraw-Hill Book Company, 1972.

New York State Department of Labor. *Guide to Preparing a Resume.* New York: New York State Employment Service, 1972.

Wolf, Morris Philip, and Robert R. Aurner. *Effective Communication in Business,* 6th ed. Cincinnati: South-Western Publishing Company, 1974.

INDEX